FALLING UP THE STAIRS

For Alan Mart, with admiration for all that you have contributed to Marin County.

Claudia Chapline 10/7/13

Claudia Chapline
A Memoir

Cover Painting:
Portrait of Claudia Chapline
by Harold Schwarm

Book Design: Prepress

Printing: Prepress, Inc.
398 Eleventh Street, 2nd Floor
San Francisco CA 94103

ISBN No. 0-9653569-7-3

Red Comma Editions
P.O. Box 1117
Stinson Beach, CA 94970
© Claudia Chapline 2013
www.claudiachapline.wordpress.com

All rights reserved.
No part of this book may be reproduced
or transmitted in any form or by any means,
electronic or mechanical, including photocopying,
recording or by an information storage and retrieval
system without written permission from the author,
except for the inclusion of brief quotations in a review.

*For my grandchildren: Marissa, Alexander, Mikaela,
Ciara and Christopher Hood*

Books by Claudia Chapline

Poetry

    Egret
    Calle Aldama
    Collage: Pop Poetry & Sound Bytes
    Sea Glass: Stinson Beach Poems

Art Catalogs

    Claudia Chapline: Selected Works
    Women Artists of Marin, editor

Contents

A Letter to my Grandchildren	5
Necessity and Invention	7
A Nuclear Family	9
Moving	18
Grandfathers	26
Birthdays	30
Harmony	32
Depression Mealtimes	34
Bat Girl	40
Can You Draw Me?	47
Jacob's Ladder	52
Petey	54
A Myopic Marriage	57
Monkey Child	62
Infant Surfer	65
Dog Stories	67
Fire in Sullivan Canyon	69
Husbands	72
My Nose in a Book	80
Learning to See	87
The Cycle of Life	89
Falling Up the Stairs	92
Home	94
Letters	97
Coat of Arms	98
Family Tree	
Chronology	
Acknowledgements	

A Letter to my Grandchildren

    This book is about a near-blind and gifted child in the Depression, a "bobby-soxer" during World War II, a postwar dancing art student, and a working mother and grandmother who lived and loved in the time of tremendous change from the industrial age to the digital age. These stories are memories of my early life in the twentieth century on the East Coast, my later life in the twenty-first century on the West Coast and the leading characters: parents, grandparents, husbands and sons.

    When I was going through my mother's things after her death, I found out that my grandmother was married in the Mormon Church and that my mother had been christened in that church. No one ever mentioned this, even though some of my school friends were Mormons. My parents didn't go to church and my sister and I walked to the nearest Protestant church for Sunday school. There were so many things about our family that my parents never told me about.

    Unlike my father who was so proud of his family's heritage, my mother never talked about her childhood or her parents and grandparents. For most of my adult life Mother and I lived on opposite coasts, so I gave her a tape recorder, hoping that she would use it to tell me her stories. But she didn't. Now I think that I should have tried harder to get her to tell me her stories during my visits at her condominium in Deland, Florida.

    Several years after my mother's death, I decided to write an autobiography. In preparation, I read many memoirs and took some classes to learn about memoir writing. The autobiography changed into a memoir that was the story of my life as an artist intertwined with stories of my family. It split into two books: a forthcoming book on my life as an artist and this book of family stories for you so you would have some answers to your questions about who and where you come from. I hope you enjoy it.

In my whole life I have attempted to live lightly on the earth. My art and writing promoted peace and justice for all and consideration for the natural environment. My generation made a mess of our dear Mother Earth and I did my best to confront negative forces with healing art. My hope is that the next generation will carry on with cultivating all that is good and beautiful.

With love to you all,

    Claudia Chapline

Necessity and Invention

A question elicits an answer. What is needed is provided. This has been my experience, from a childhood in Illinois and Virginia and college days in Washington, D.C. to adulthood in Missouri and California. During the 1930s Depression we wore hand-me-down clothes but we always had enough to eat, a bicycle for riding to school and the Encyclopedia Britannica to help with homework. Our parents loved us but were strict disciplinarians so we stayed away from them as much as possible. After school was our time for running and playing and exploring the woods and town. We were free to find for ourselves what our parents couldn't provide — a familiarity with the natural world and its creatures, skills at the recreation center and books at the local library. Our secret adventures ended at dark when we had to be home for dinner.

My father died when I was nineteen. But he had provided an encouraging example when I was a child, as he moved from job to job after his contracting business failed in the crash of 1929. He was an engineer and an inventor. He taught my sister and me that we could solve problems, fix broken things and create what we could envision.

He showed us a model of an invention that would lay hot asphalt cold. In the basement he ran gravel through a cardboard tube in the big double sink. This was the era of building the country's infrastructure, creating highways for the automobiles that were replacing travel by train and streetcar.

As I grew into a young adult, jobs were easy to find. Though I had no social skills, I was artistic and confident in my ability to find work and to do a good job. I had started teaching dance in after-school programs during my teenage years. While in college, I did office work during the week, taught art to children on Saturdays and worked as a camp counselor in the summers, teaching dance and drama. After graduation, there were instructor positions to choose from. And after marriage, teaching jobs came my way as I followed my husband from St. Louis to Columbia, Missouri to Los Angeles, to Eureka and back to Los Angeles. All along the way, I made art — paintings, dances and poems – no matter how little money, space or time I had.

I furnished our houses and clothed the children from thrift shops. Once, when riding my bicycle down an alley in Santa Monica, I saw a brand new pair of tennis shoes in my size on top of a trashcan. They were just what I'd been dreaming about. It seemed that thinking about a need produced the desired object. I found dance studios this way as well as art supplies, and sneakers.

Once I needed some rubber tubing to complete an art object. Instead of going to the hardware store, I went to the beach and found what I needed in the exact diameter and length necessary.

These experiences continued when I moved to Stinson Beach with my second husband and started an art gallery. Somehow I always earned what was necessary to keep it going. I am grateful for the lucky star over my head and the angels – or whatever it is that rewards faith and hard work – who have helped me live a creative life.

A Nuclear Family

Lying on my back in the wicker baby carriage, I could feel the wind off Lake Michigan on my face. Overhead was the El, its black lines against a gray sky. When the train went by it was exciting. My mother said that Daddy taught me to whistle. People were surprised to hear a baby whistling.

The bright lights of the Christmas tree high above my small body were dazzling. From their bright centers the lights' rays merged into magical halos. Standing there and looking up, I was enthralled by the glows of red, blue, green and yellow bulbs. The room was dark and the tree was dark in the spaces between the halos. Daddy swooped me up into his arms. He held me high, so high, as I put the star on the top of the tree. I was two and I was shining. This was my most memorable Christmas. From that day on, I painted and colored books with crayons, and wore red dresses with pockets.

I had not yet come into loving, so when they brought Shirley home from the hospital I didn't like her. But then what two-year-old likes a little sister? Everyone thought she was so cute but I couldn't see it. She was red skinned and a crybaby. As time went by we could play together, but I always had to watch out for her.

What can a three year old do when it is raining? Mother handed me a pencil and a small rainbow memo pad. She said, "You can draw." Once I started drawing, I never stopped. I loved making black marks on the pastel hued paper and I still love mark making on any surface and enjoy brush drawing and incorporating writing into paintings. Drawing was to become one with the thing seen – drawing water, drawing the path of my life, the face of another's thoughts, drawing the melody of breath.

From an early age I loved to run. I ran so fast that my parents had to huff and puff to catch me when I was small. Running through fields of flowers was delightful. I loved the feeling of the air rushing by my ears, my hair blowing and the sense of freedom and speed. I twirled until dizzy and rolled down hills, practiced somersaults and played dodge ball, hopscotch and jump rope all summer. It was the beginning of the love of motion that impelled me to become a dancer and in later years to draw dancers to incorporate motion into my visual work.

Daddy took me the Chicago Exposition when I was four. I wanted to ride on the Ferris wheel. It was higher than a two-story house. Daddy gave me a penny to put in a machine. The penny came out flat and changed into an ellipse. It was magical. I put it in my pocket where it was treasured for many years.

Just for the excitement, I wanted to run away from home when I was five, but I didn't want to go alone. I tried to talk Shirley into going with me. We were at the corner on our tricycles in Oak Park, Illinois. But she was afraid, afraid of everything. She said she couldn't go because she wasn't allowed to cross the street by herself.

Shirley was accident-prone. When we were a little bit older, she fell through a sheet of glass that covered seedlings. There was blood all over her leg from a huge cut. I ran home, and told Mother, who came running. She picked up Shirley and wrapped her leg in towels and then took her to the hospital in a taxi. Afterwards, Shirley had a deep scar the length of her thigh.

One day I walked into a big, strange room. The crayons were bigger than my fingers – pink, green and turquoise. They lay on a huge pale green circular table surrounded by child-sized chairs. The first day of kindergarten was my best day so far – until naptime. I didn't nap at home and I certainly was not going to nap there. Naps had been discontinued after I escaped a locked room upstairs by climbing out of the window and sliding down the porch roof's support, and Mother caught me playing on the lawn. So, the teacher said that I could just sit on the mat and read. "Just be quiet."

Later, in school, teachers let me go to the library so that I wouldn't disturb the other children by talking. As I got older, I noticed that my mother and sister chattered constantly. Everything they thought came out of their mouths. I couldn't get a word in sideways and besides, they sounded stupid to me with all that jabbering about nothing. I clammed up and never really learned to converse with pleasure, even after speech and acting classes, teaching and performing. I was fine as long as I had an outline or a script of what to say, but I just froze up in social situations. Finally, owning an art gallery taught me to talk with strangers about anything.

My parents were strict disciplinarians. One of my first lessons was to tell the truth no matter what. When I was about three, I climbed up onto the kitchen counter and opened up a package of Oreo cookies from a high shelf. After licking out the sweet white insides, I put the cookies back together and carefully replaced them in the package and returned it to its place on the shelf. Mother would never know, I thought. But Mother did know. She asked, "Claudia, you have ruined these cookies. The white centers are gone. What happened?" "I don't know," I lied. "They must have come that way from the store." Boy, did I get a licking. Not for eating the cookies but for lying about it.

With my independent, creative and adventurous spirit, my parents always had something to complain about. I was well into adulthood before I stopped cringing when someone called me by my name. In those early years, when my parents said "Claudia," it meant a lesson, a chastisement, a spanking with a hair brush by Mother, or a whipping by Daddy — with his razor strap for serious infractions. At that time spanking was not considered to be child abuse; it was the way many parents taught their children to behave. I learned to avoid my parents by going to my friends' houses, wandering in the woods, playing outside until dark or, when indoors, by reading books. Later, playing the piano and singing were also ways to isolate myself from parental demands.

Not all Christmases were joyful. My father was drinking. Mother, my little sister Shirley and I, were always packing up and leaving. But we always came back. In 1934 when I was four, Shirley, and I were in a boarding school. Shirley got chickenpox and we had to stay there for Christmas because of the quarantine. How we hated that place. A skinny old witch with a frowning mouth and dyed black hair ran the school. She put pepper on our tongues when we said bad words. The oatmeal was not as good as Mother's and the stewed prunes at breakfast were disgusting. So was the latrine that smelled of wet cement and more. I became aware of the smell of my own waste. I wanted to run away but there was no way out, only reading books at night with the light that came from under and around the closed door. Back at home when I complained about that time, mother told me that it was a very good boarding school. I didn't think any boarding school could be good.

In the backyard of our house in Washington, D.C. there was a wall. A cemetery was on the other side. When Mother wasn't looking, my sister Shirley and I climbed over the wall. The grass was truly greener on the other side and there were flowers and tombstones to run around. We spent many happy hours playing there when I was six. One day I met a nice woman there who showed me how to make baskets by cutting and weaving strips of paper. That chance meeting opened a door for me. I made Easter baskets for my family and friends with scrap paper. From then on I made all sorts of things with paper – doll clothes, cards, books, sculptures and later, window installations and books. I still love paper and as an adult often paint with ink on Japanese papers, and make collages and unique artist's books as well as occasional paper sculptures.

My sister Shirley and I loved our maternal grandmother, Leuzetta Schell Hartman. We spent my sixth summer reading movie magazines and listening to the ladies gossiping in Grandmother's beauty salon on the side of her large house in Oak Park. I remember the acrid smells of vinegar, permanent wave solutions and singed hair from curling irons. Grandma was tall and hump-shouldered from years of bending over blued heads. The bluing kept grey hair from turning yellow. Her ankles were swollen from standing on her feet all day. She smelled of sweet, scented powder. We called her Mama Lou.

She formed our straight hair into sausage curls with a curling iron. Shirley Temple was the model at that time. "Claudia would be such a pretty girl, if only her hair were curly," Mama Lou said. Shortly after I went out to play, my curls straightened out. That might be one of the reasons I grew up thinking that I was ugly — in contrast to my little sister, who got all the compliments. Her curls stayed in longer than mine and I was too blind to see myself.

In Mama Lou's big old house, Shirley and I played the grand piano that was usually covered with a paisley shawl. The living room was dark, with the heavy drapes closed. When we played cat and dog fight or thunderstorm and hail on the piano Mama Lou would come rushing out from the beauty salon, shouting "Hark, hark, your noise!" We giggled and went down into the cellar to turn wheels: the knife sharpener's huge round stone was grey and gritty and the wringer washer's white rubber rollers looked dangerous to our small fingers. But we spun them anyway.

Mama Lou gave me a little loom, four inches square, called Weave-It. I wove squares with a skein of variegated yarn that she sewed into an afghan. I loved the gradation of colors. Where did one color end and another color begin? How did yellow become orange and change into red, blue into purple, green into turquoise? Beginnings and endings became a life-long study as I tried to see where one thing ended and another thing began. I spent many hours studying the auras of people and objects. Since I could not see edges I became interested in interfaces, the in between spaces of everything.

I was highly myopic, everything I saw was out of focus so I learned things by color, placement and movement. I also whiled away summer afternoons watching the black floaters in my eyes and the dust motes floating in the light. White specks merged with black specks. At night I slept in Grandmother's big brass bed in the attic that was covered with crazy quilts. I felt like a princess in a fairy tale. The dark red, blue and green satin triangles, decoratively sewn together with orange and pink embroidery threads were smooth and warm on my skin. It wasn't long before the sandman came and I was off to dreamland where, drifting in a floating continuum, the dark rich colors of night revealed pieces of puzzles.

Mama Lou's second husband, Daddy Will, took me to see a prizefight. The huge hall, the smoke and the noise are an indelible memory. I didn't see much of the fighting because it was too far away and I didn't like the idea of men punching each other anyway.

Breakfast at Mama Lou's was homemade cookies served on dishes printed with pictures of windmills, and Shirley and I could have all the milk we wanted to drink. After breakfast we ran off to the swimming pool. On Saturdays we went to the movies, where we ate sugar daddies and licorice ropes while watching *Blood on the Sand* or horror movies.

The train ride home from Chicago to Washington, D.C. (where my family was now living) on the Streamliner was great fun. We ate cookies all day and slept in the upper berth at night. When we got home we had to settle for a healthy breakfast and only one glass of milk. Mother said that Grandmother had spoiled us.

I never met my paternal grandmother, Alice Hodges Chapline. She grew up on her father's plantation in Mississippi. At the age of nine she was an expert horse-rider. At thirteen she was sent to a fashionable boarding school for girls. She grew into a hardy woman who, while wearing the long skirts of her generation, organized the women in Sarasota to build the first boardwalk. She had eight children including one daughter who died in infancy. Well into her nineties she lived alone and took care of her house until she fell off a ladder while changing curtains. I wonder how many women have met their end this way?

On the first day of first grade I was both excited and apprehensive. When the teacher saw that I could read and print well, she sent me upstairs to the next class. The teacher was explaining opposites and I liked that idea. Noticing that everything on the blackboard was in handwriting. I was forced to quickly learn handwriting. We were told to tilt our papers to the right, or was it the left? It was confusing because I am left-handed, so I did it the way everyone else did.

Our eyes were tested and I flunked. I could tell there was an E on the top of the chart because the examiner said so. All the letters were Es because some of the children were slow with letters. We were instructed to point three fingers in the direction of the Es that we saw. I couldn't see any of them. They gave me a half sheet of yellow paper to take to my parents for another eye exam. I knew what that meant – glasses. There was a little boy on our block who wore glasses. He was always falling off his tricycle and all the children teased him. Letting the paper blow away across a field on my way home from school was the end of it, I thought. When the school tested our eyesight the next year I watched the children in front of me and memorized the directions of their hand movements. Adams and Brown came before Chapline so I passed the eye exam even though I couldn't see the letters on the eye chart.

From then on I always sat in the front row. In order to read the blackboard for tests, I would break my pencil, walk across the front while reading the questions on the way to the pencil sharpener, review it on the way back to my seat and still finish answering all the questions before any one else. I had to work quickly while I remembered the questions. Reading was so difficult that I developed a photographic memory. Once I read something, I could remember the page and its content.

I often wonder why so many artists have visual difficulties, why musicians have hearing problems and dancers have body problems. Is it because they overuse their preferred faculties or have they become the kind of artists they are because of certain limitations? Perhaps taking so many pains to develop as an artist is a compensation for a sensed weakness in some area of perception. Once I had glasses I no longer needed a photographic memory so it gradually left me.

The memories of second grade at Matthew F. Maury Elementary School include the day of the color pencil robbery. Another girl came to school with a brand new set of Mongol pencils in a folding box. Every color was there. I couldn't stand it. She wasn't an artist. I was an artist and I thought my parents could never afford to buy me anything like that. Somehow, at the end of the school day, I stole that box of colored pencils and hid them somewhere. The next day the whole school was talking about the terrible thing that had happened. Now I was feeling awful. I couldn't return the pencils because of my shame, and I couldn't use them for fear of detection and my feelings of guilt. I broke the pencils in half, chewed on them and rubbed them in the dirt to make them look old. Even with all that effort, I never enjoyed drawing with the stolen pencils. The beautiful colors were forever dimmed by shame, even though no one knew of my crime. Had I been a Catholic, I would have confessed, returned the pencils, apologized and not be writing this now.

Moving

Between first grade in Washington D.C. and third grade in Arlington, Virginia, I went to a number of different schools. We were following Daddy's FHA jobs in various cities. In Newport News, Virginia, the maid, Viola, sewed doll clothes and taught us to play card games like Old Maid and Rummy when Mother went shopping. Shortly before Mother's return, we would quit playing and Viola would hurriedly vacuum the rug while Shirley and I dusted the furniture. In St. Petersburg, Virginia, Mother slipped on the waxed floor of our rented house and chipped the end of her spine. She had to lie upstairs on a board all summer. Shirley and I took advantage of her absence and had fun playing with the pet rabbits in the large grassy back yard. It was a relaxed summer of freedom from Mother's supervision and criticism.

Moving for me was always the start of a new adventure. I learned to make friends quickly but not to become too close. The constant moving was harder on Shirley. In Lynchburg, Virginia, a city of many hills, I learned to roller skate. That was a year of scabby knees and elbows. The skates were clamped onto the soles of my shoes and tightened with a skate key that I wore around my neck. As the clamps loosened, many an ecstatic downhill ride ended in a crash when a skate fell off my shoe or the skate got caught in a sidewalk crack and I went flying into the street.

One day, on my way home from school I went into a side door of an old brick church covered with ivy. Inside there was a beautiful spiral staircase. I eagerly climbed up it to find myself in front of an organ. How wonderful, I thought. Then I sat down and began playing the keyboard, pulling out knobs, and making the most powerful sounds of heavenly music, so I thought. My joy was interrupted when the minister came up the staircase. He asked me if I liked to sing and invited me to join the choir. And that is how I became a Presbyterian and started singing.

We lived in an apartment building in Lynchburg, Virginia and I played with the janitor's son who was about my age. His cat had kittens and he gave me a sweet little white one. When I took it upstairs to our apartment, the kitten climbed up the lace curtains, tearing them into shreds. Mother was furious and made me return the kitten. My parents said I shouldn't play with that boy any more because he was black. I didn't understand why that was a good reason. After all, his father, like mine, had a degree in engineering, though he had to work as a janitor. I returned the kitten and my friend's father said he understood, and that I would understand when I grew up. I still don't understand.

When I was eight we moved again, to Arlington, Virginia, which was a new suburb. The Virginia long pole pine forest was cut down to make room for building the apartments where we lived. In the backyard squirrels scurried up and down the remaining pine trees. The new school was Kate Waller Barrett, located about half a mile from our apartment on North Henderson Road. The area is now a historic district. Back then I liked to wander in the pine forest surrounding the school's playground before and after school, to learn about the plants and animals that lived there – beavers, butterflies and moths, Dogwood trees and Jack in the Pulpits. It was here that Mother said that Daddy could work anywhere he wanted to, but she would not move for another five years. In fact, she didn't move for over twenty years.

Our parents bought bicycles, red for me and blue for my sister Shirley so that we could ride to school. Among the first things that I learned were that no one likes a smart kid and that girls were not supposed to be smart. So I never raised my hand in school and always finished my homework in school. My third grade teacher, Miss Shepherd, let me draw with chalk on the sidewall of the classroom. As the other children finished, they joined me in coloring in my mural. Sometimes the wall was covered with tan paper for painting.

Miss Shepherd was beautiful. She had shoulder length brown hair and large brown eyes. She wore a shiny blouse printed with a brilliantly striped pattern of black, gold, red and green. I had never seen colors like that on fabric before. Miss Shepherd said it was a Roman Stripe pattern. She gave us a lesson in writing poetry with meter and rhyme and one of my poems was published in the Washington Post. A visiting art teacher came once a month, teaching us about shading and perspective. I practiced her lessons all month and eagerly waited for the next lesson. My friend, Jenonne Jacques and I had reading races to see who could read the most books in a week. I read everything in the school library, then everything in the small public library. There wasn't that much to offer at the new suburban library beyond Nancy Drew Girl Detective stories.

Seeing his duty to educate his children, Daddy drove us in the black Ford on Sunday outings to cemeteries in Virginia. We looked at tombstones at Gettysburg, cannons at Appomattox or the changing of the guard at Arlington Cemetery. But the visits to the museums in Washington, D.C. were my favorite outings. I remember none of the battlefields, but Corot's nymphs still dance in a green forest and Van Gogh's blues and oranges still vibrate in my mind.

My mother, despite her youth, decades younger than my father, was better than my father at coping with the family's changed circumstances during the Depression. As a young child she lived on a farm in Michigan until her father died in an accident and her mother, my grandmother, moved to Oak Park, Illinois. Grandmother supported her two children by managing a beauty school attached to the house. Stella, my mother, took care of her little brother, Lyle, and helped Grandmother with housework. As a teenager, she helped in the shop by modeling hairstyles, doing the bookkeeping and shopping for supplies. She was petite, beautiful and very feminine. She finished high school at the age of sixteen, married my father when she was seventeen and became a very good housekeeper and money manager.

In her early twenties with two young children to care for, she was distressed by financial problems. She didn't want any more children so she went to a doctor to find out about the latest methods of birth control. This was a big step for her. A friend who was a Christian Scientist had introduced her to those teachings. So, instead of going to doctors for illness Mother read Christian Science literature. She didn't allow our dentist to use painkillers and, unlike most of our friends, we did not have our tonsils removed.

Mother always had more than one of everything – multiples of shoes and purses to match her many outfits. Each purse had a compact, lipstick, tissues, pen, memo pad and whatever else she needed every day. That saved time because it took her a very long time to get dressed. She was always perfectly groomed and would not leave the house unless she was dressed to the nines. It all started with bras and girdles, then slips and stockings before getting to the outer garments. She and her closets were perfectly organized. I think keeping her things in perfect order kept her from falling into despair. She often lay on her bed, quietly crying. I never knew why. Daddy said, "Your mother has only one fault. She is never on time."

For Shirley and me, Mother had our cousins' outgrown clothes altered to fit us. Sometimes it was embarrassing, like the time I had to wear a striped fuzzy coat that made me feel like a big skunk. People were into furs and animal clothes then. Mother said it was a good coat because it was expensive. I felt so ugly in that coat, especially when we had to line up for a family picture in our winter clothes.

We had new clothes for Easter and for the beginning of school each fall. By the time Easter came, my feet had grown and the black patent leather Mary Jane shoes Mother had bought for me months earlier were too small. People walked around after church on Easter Sunday so that everyone could admire their new clothes. We had bows in our hair, ruffled dresses, Easter hats, white gloves and socks, and the new shiny shoes that pinched my toes. Grandmother had a black sealskin coat and hat. Mother had a stole of little foxes with fascinating jaw clips – they bit their tails to stay put on Mother's shoulders. Mother's friend, Mrs. Provost, let us play on her polar bear rug when we went to her house for tea and cookies. The huge bear had glass eyes and sharp teeth. And just inside the door there was a life-sized sculpture of a black Scottie. Animals were everywhere!

One of my earliest memories is of my mother pushing her Bissell, a carpet sweeper, on the floor. She had a Bissell as soon as she became a housewife, replacing them every twenty years as they wore out. Each time they looked smaller to me. In her later years she had an upstairs Bissell and a downstairs Bissell so that she wouldn't have to carry one up and down the stairs.

Even when I was in middle age, my ever-thoughtful mother sent me a Bissell after visiting me, and the dust balls on my carpets. I made sure to use it before her every visit. She even sent me two vacuum cleaners after she updated her cleaning equipment. In her eighties she was shrinking and so she got a smaller vacuum cleaner – a Mighty Mite, lest no mites take up residence in her house.

My father, Jacob Burwell Chapline II, known as Jake, was born in Little Rock, Arkansas in 1876. His parents were pioneers in the settlement of Sarasota, Florida, where my Grandfather, Jacob Burwell Chapline, was a circuit court judge. The Chapline family goes back in the USA to 1610 when Isaac Chapline arrived on the *Starr* from England. Daddy was very proud of the family history. He had a degree in engineering and was an inventor who lost his construction business in the crash of 1929. When we were young he worked for the Federal Housing Authority (FHA) as an inspector of low-income housing projects. Since we moved frequently I got used to going to a new school every six months, but my sister never did. At various times I attended the Methodist, Presbyterian or Episcopalian Church. When I was old enough to choose, I went to the church with the best music. Music was important to me because of my visual handicap. I was very near sighted, so much so that everything beyond three feet away from me was a blur. I sang in church choirs from eight to eighteen. By then I was more interested in Eastern religions and could no longer accept some of the Christian doctrines that made no sense to me. Art became my spiritual practice.

When I was nine the Encyclopedia Britannica, bound in burgundy leather with gold lettering, arrived at our house for Christmas. My decision to read the whole encyclopedia kept me busy. The slick black and white illustrations of the ancient Greek male statues were a turn-on to my incipient sexuality. The next Christmas, a set of green leather bound literary classics was the family present. The books were stored in a rotating drum table in the living room. The author's names were imprinted with gold lettering on the three-inch thick volumes. From then on I was greatly influenced by the essays of Henry David Thoreau, Ralph Waldo Emerson and the poetry of Walt Whitman and Emily Dickinson. I also enjoyed the stories of Nathaniel Hawthorne, Edgar Allen Poe, Emile Zola and Guy De Maupassant.

Books became a way out of the racism of my father, my perceived limitations of my mother's life as a housewife, and my own optical deficiency. During the summer, I read the entire King James Version of the Holy Bible, a 1939 confirmation present. I read about the explorers in South America among the Jivaros and in the mountains of Tibet. I was interested in anthropology but knew that I could not cross hanging bridges over rivers in the jungle. I told my parents that I wanted to go to Lhasa to visit the Dalai Llama. With my genetic inheritance as an asthmatic I would not be comfortable at that altitude, but I didn't know that then. My interest in Tibet persisted in my reading but by the time I had grown up and could afford to go, the Tibet I wanted to see no longer existed.

In junior high school we were assigned our first term papers. Mine was about the history of comic strips. Another paper was on the remnants of English ballads in the Appalachian Mountains. The Library of Congress was a great resource and I felt very grown up by going to

D.C. from Arlington on the bus and sitting in the library's dark room along with nuns at the long wooden tables. Pete Seeger's Collection of Appalachian music was one of the great treasures there that I loved. No one censored my requests. I could read anything I wanted to, for example, Cocteau or De Quincey's *Confessions of an Opium Eater* etc. By the time I had read many books about all kinds of drugs, I had no desire to experiment with my sensitive body, feeling that enhanced perception, visions and hallucinations are experiences of the mind that are available to any person.

When I was attending classes at The George Washington University, I dated a doctoral candidate in American History who had a private desk in the stacks. So it was that the Library of Congress became a place for romance in life rather than in novels. But the books always lasted longer than the boyfriends and the romances.

I have always been interested in short forms because they are condensed and say the most with the least. I prefer novellas to novels, chamber music to symphonies, lyric rather than epic verse. I was influenced by the poetry of Emily Dickinson, Basho, Pablo Neruda, and Octavio Paz.

As a youth, I enjoyed the chamber music concerts and poetry readings at the Phillips Gallery in Washington, D.C. that they held on weekend afternoons. There I could see art at the same time. The paintings that I saw so many times live in my memory more than the music or poetry that I heard only once. Sitting at the front on the left side, I could look at El Greco's *View of Toledo* on the wall directly in front of me. To the left of the grand piano was Rouault's *Old King*, a magnificent painting that I didn't understand for many years.

Grandfathers

Grandfather Daniel Schell, my mother's father, was so cold that Michigan night on the farm. He went out to the garage to warm up the car. He didn't hear the wind shut the door. The car was warm then and he was drowsy. Who found him there too late? What did he look like then? What did he do before taking that last ride to nowhere? Why are there no pictures, no memorabilia, no memory, nothing but a hole in time and unanswered questions that only a Mormon librarian might answer? I did not know he was Mormon until after my mother's death when I found my Grandmother's wedding certificate.

Great Grandfather Beechum, my grandmother's father, had a strong benign presence, standing there under convex glass in an oval frame, his generous moustache curling so handsomely. He was a debonair gentleman to be sure. So why was he hung up in the closet?

Grandfather Jacob Burwell Chapline, my father's father, also lived in the closet, his image on a tintype framed in red velvet. He was only sixteen, a proud miniature standing in a full-dress Confederate uniform. Where did his picture go when Daddy died and Mother remarried and changed her name from Chapline to Raines?

I was named for my aunt Claudia Chapline who died of yellow fever. Claudia is the feminine of the Latin, Claudius (lame). I also wear my grandfathers' names, the North and the South coexisting, gravel and grits in a mid-western twang. The name Chapline is English and French for keeper of the king's chapel. My middle name, Beechum, is for my maternal grandfather, who died before I was born, and whose portrait I saw in the closet. The name Beechum comes from beech, a tree. Perhaps that is why I feel a kinship with the Druids, who worshipped trees. In medieval times, beech wood was used for the covers of large books. The word beech, in German, is *bucke*, the origin of the English word, book. Next to art, I love books. Chapline is English-French for keeper of the king's chapel. Am I the Anglo-Saxon sister of Kokapeli, the hump-backed flute player of the Hopi? He makes music out of his burden. I make visual music out of my concerns.

My parents never called me by my name unless I had done something to provoke their criticism. That is why I didn't like to hear my name for many years, even though I knew it wasn't a label. It was a caring that I didn't recognize. It took many years for me to get used to my name, my face, my voice and my body. For similar reasons I had difficulty in addressing people by their names. It was also because my extreme myopia made it difficult for me to recognize people's faces. Everything beyond three feet was a blur. I recognized people by their voices and their movements.

Claudia Chapline at 6 Months
1930

Claudia Chapline at 3
1933

Claudia Chapline at 13
1943

Claudia Chapline at 21
1951

Judge Jacob Burwell Chapline
(Grandfather) with (Grandmother) Alice

Leuzetta Beecham Schell
(Grandmother)

Lillian Estella Schell at 17
(Mother)

Jacob Burwell Chapline II
(Father)

Birthdays

My parents couldn't give me art lessons but for birthdays they gave me art supplies. For my tenth birthday there was a watercolor set in a black metal box. I painted flowers: roses and irises. The watercolors are long gone but I made a sculpture with the metal box. On my eleventh birthday the present was a wooden box with pastels in many colors. I still have the box and some fragments of the pastels. I did so many chalk paintings at school that I was continually coughing from the dust. After that I preferred wet media to dry media.

One Sunday while wandering in the park, I came across a painter. He gave me a canvas and showed me how to paint with oils. When I proudly took my small, completed canvas home, my parents said I shouldn't talk to men in the park. For my next birthday the present was an oil painting set complete with an instruction book and easel. My parents knew nothing about art, but they provided me with good art materials.

These presents were wonderful but I wanted so badly to have a birthday party like my friends did. After much begging my mother gave in and I had a birthday party with a giant chocolate-covered strawberry shortcake. When she asked me what kind of cake I wanted, that was what I suggested. It was a beautiful birthday but Mother cried the whole next day. I thought the effort of preparing for the party was too much for her so I never asked for a birthday party again.

I forgot about birthdays until I was fifty. That was a low year in my life. My studio was closed and I had lost my source of income from teaching because of a prohibitive rent increase for the studio. I wanted to invite all of my friends to a party and give them a gift for my birthday. When the time came, I didn't have money for invitations or refreshments, so I spent the day alone, cutting three feet of hair off of my head. The more I cut, the lighter I felt. Since then I wear my hair short and only note the birthdays ending in zero. On these occasions I invite a few close friends to share dinner.

  A memorable birthday did come later in my life when I was cruising with my son, Randall, in the Galapagos Islands. A sea lion followed the boat – waving. In the wood-paneled dining rooms there were pyramids of pineapples, mangoes, guavas and melons. Song surrounded me and I was draped with balloons. I cut tiers of chocolate cake tall enough for a wedding party. I blew out the candles wishing never to anchor and always to keep my spiritual balloon high. My son gave me a book of photographs of blue-footed boobies, colorful fish, and giant sea turtles. The sea lion kept following the boat – waving.

Harmony

Somehow my parents managed to give me music lessons with Alma Grayce Miller, a composer. Since I was always creative with any medium, I composed a piece about the sound of church bells. Miss Miller showed me how to correct it according to the rules of harmony. The problem was that she removed the dissonances I liked and forced me to play the amended composition in the annual recital. That was the end of my interest in music composition, though I continued to study piano with her until I graduated from high school. When I decided to concentrate on painting and dance in college, she was very disappointed because I had been her star pupil, and she had hoped I would go to Juilliard School of Music. But I knew that I did not have perfect pitch and that my hands were not large. She thought I was talented because I could play after going through the sheet music one time. But that was really because I had developed a photographic memory in compensation for my poor vision. It was so much effort to read the music that I knew it by heart after once figuring it out.

I had asked my parents many times for piano lessons, art lessons and dancing lessons. Mother said, "Ladies don't dance." There were so many things that ladies didn't do that I had no desire to become one when I grew up. According to my mother, ladies spoke softly, didn't take big steps, climb trees, or get master's degrees. They got married and had children, period.

My mother gave me a nickel for graham crackers and milk each day in the third grade. I saved the nickels until Friday when I could go to the recreation center and buy a ballet lesson for twenty-five cents. The teacher's dress was faded black and she hit our legs with a cane to correct our positions. For stretching our legs we used the windowsill instead of a *barre* for support.

Determined to learn any way I could, I also met my friends on their way home from dancing lessons. They showed me the steps they had learned that day and I practiced them until the next week's lesson. I began composing dances for my friends and myself. We performed the dances at our mothers' garden parties and at the Home for Veterans on an outdoor stage, surrounded by old men in wheel chairs on the lawn. We did ballets and folk dances that I arranged from steps I learned from my friends and from books in the library. Our mothers made our costumes.

By the age of twelve I had more freedom and bus money. On Saturdays I could take the bus from Arlington to Washington D.C. and go to the Smithsonian Museums and the Library of Congress where I could research more folk dances. One teenage summer I attended a folkdance camp in the Shenandoah Mountains where I learned more about Appalachian folk music and folk tales.

A few years later, my friend Joan Higginson invited me to go with her family to see Martha Graham perform at the Lisner Auditorium in D.C. This was a turning point in my life, the first time I had seen or even heard of modern dance. What I saw was incredible — Cave of the Heart, Lamentation, Every Soul is a Circus, and Appalachian Spring with music by Aaron Copland and set sculptures by Isamu Noguchi. This was a creative integration of poetry, art, music and dance. I didn't understand modern dance at the time but I knew it was a direction I needed to follow.

Depression Mealtimes

When we lived in Arlington, Virginia, sometimes in the spring cherry blossom time, we went to D.C. to picnic under weeping willow trees along the Potomac River. Or on the Fourth of July we spread a plaid blanket on the grass surrounding the Washington Monument to enjoy the national fireworks display. While waiting for dark, Shirley and I collected fireflies in jars for lanterns.

Most of the time we ate dinner at home. Mother wasn't a very good cook even though she thought a lot about it. She tried hard but the toast was always burnt and the meat overdone. Like me, she was also very nearsighted, and would not wear glasses because of her vanity. But the food usually looked better than it tasted. Even the family breakfast table was properly set. My favorite breakfast was rice pudding made from last night's leftovers. My least-favorite breakfast was grits. My father loved grits. He told us to think about the starving children in China and be happy that we had something to eat. Mornings were better when we had scrambled eggs and bacon. During the Second World War we had ration stamps for food, and grew kale in our Victory garden. It was one of the few vegetables we had that didn't come out of a can. We collected newspapers, tin foil from cigarette packages and scrap metal as our part of the war effort.

Once a week, a farmer walked on our street calling out "Fresh Eggs, Apples!" When we heard him, Shirley and I would run out to buy some. In the summers, Shirley and I would run outside to buy ice cream sandwiches and popsicles when we heard the Good Humor man's bell ring.

During World War II the only bananas we could find in the store were big green Cuban bananas. My Mother loved bananas and insisted that we eat the slimy things because they were good for us. They made me gag and I felt like throwing up with every bite. They were almost as bad as orange juice with castor oil.

Once I left home I never, well almost never, ate bananas. Well, not until I was married to Harold and he put bananas on the granola for breakfast. I learned to tolerate an almost ripe half banana in small slices as the price to pay for his making the breakfast. As long as there are no brown spots or slimy edges I will eat bananas for the potassium they contain. I got along fine for decades without bananas. For me, the best way to eat bananas is with chocolate ice cream.

School lunches were a sliced lunchmeat sandwich, an apple, and a carrot that mother said was good for my eyes. After school I was a latchkey child struggling to get the key that hung from a string around my neck. I was about to wet my pants when I unlocked the apartment's door. There was a peanut butter and jelly sandwich and a glass of milk on the kitchen counter. Where was my Mother? She must have gone shopping with Shirley, but she never told me, and the answer is buried with Mother. She didn't work outside the home. She had no car, so she called in the groceries and sent the dirty clothes out to the Chinese laundry. I often ate alone and listened on the radio to Jack Armstrong the All American Boy, the Lone Ranger or The Shadow before going out to play with my friends. I was good at hopscotch and jump rope, and loved dodge ball because I was quick on my feet and often won. I could always see the big ball in time to catch it – not like in softball where I always missed that little ball. After the sidewalk games we played hide and seek or cops and robbers until dark, when we had to be home in time to wash up for dinner.

We four, Mother, Daddy, Shirley and I sat around the oval mahogany dining table with flaring legs. The smooth polished wood was always covered with a white tablecloth. Shirley and I set the table with the red chrysanthemum patterned china. During the week, dinner might be Kraft macaroni and cheese, meat loaf, creamed chipped beef on toast, fried Spam, chicken *a la* king, black-eyed peas cooked with ham hocks or very tough fried liver and onions. Crispy pork chops were a rare treat. Usually there was some lettuce or a tomato slice with French dressing, potatoes or rice, Wonder Bread and butter, milk and, sometimes, chocolate pudding for dessert. On weekends we often had dried-up stringy roast beef, beef stew with dumplings, or fried chicken and biscuits. We had turkey for Thanksgiving with yams, dressing and pumpkin pie.

There was always plenty to eat but we were not allowed to waste a bite. We could help ourselves to as much as we wanted but we had to eat everything we put on our plates. "Waste not, want not," Daddy said. As I lifted my fork for the last bite Mother scooped up the dish. She was very proud of her perfect housekeeping.

Dinner was the time for parental instruction on table manners: Chew with your mouth closed, keep your hands in your lap, keep your head over your plate, do not play with your food. I would gaze at the reproduction of an Arkansas landscape painting on the wall.

Daddy was a Southerner and Mother was a Northerner, but she became a Southern lady after marrying my father. She even spoke with a Southern accent and acquired racist attitudes. We lived with reproductions of Colonial furniture. From family visits to museums I was aware of the difference between originals and reproductions. At eleven I lacked an appreciation of my Mother's efforts to make a beautiful home environment. This was the beginning of my critical attitude toward everything.

    My parent's rules were never to discuss religion, sex or politics at the table. Dinner was a time for stories about our day. Daddy told *Uncle Remus* stories that he remembered from his childhood in the south, such as *Brer Rabbit and the Tar Baby*. These were Afro-American folk tales about animals. Brer Rabbit was always successful in tricking Brer Fox who wanted to catch him for his dinner. But the most interesting stories were about Daddy's youth in Arkansas, like the time he got lost in dense thickets of cane, or canoeing in the swamp with the black boy who served as his companion and servant, or the time his horse bucked because of a snake in the grass, throwing him onto a rock that broke his back. The horse stayed beside him until a man came along, wondering why a horse was standing alone in the prairie. He found Jake, got help and took him to the hospital. I hope someone rewarded the horse for saving Daddy's life.

    Following the stories, Daddy led us in playing mathematical games in our heads. When dinner was over, Shirley and I helped Mother with the dishes. Daddy sat in his lounge chair, his feet up on the chintz-covered footstool, his smoking stand by his side, chain-smoking Lucky Strike cigarettes, while listening to Walter Winchell's news programs on the radio. The news was of the Depression, strikes and riots, the drought in Oklahoma, the Second World War. But inside Mother's living room, Mother and Daddy sat in their special slip covered chairs that were protected by white-crocheted doilies on the arms and backs. And we children did our best "to be seen and not heard."

There was an alley with many flowers not far from our house. The old black preacher who lived there behind a white picket fence came out and spoke with me one day when I was walking by and looking with fascination at his yard which was filled with many sculptures made from scraps of metal, wood and cement. This was my first exposure to folk sculpture, an experience that fed into my later interest in all kinds of folk art, folk dance and folk tales. When I told my parents about my wonderful discovery, they said I should not go down the alleys and not talk to black people any more. I didn't understand but I had to obey them. Still, the racist inoculation by my Southern father did not take with me. Reading Richard Wright's *Native Son* a few years later gave me words with which to confront my father's racism. For two years I tried to change him. He also spoke negatively about all the immigrants - the Polish, the Jews, the Italians, the Irish. I cringed when I think of the names he called anyone who wasn't like himself. Finally realizing that he would never stop being a "Red Neck," I stopped wasting my time arguing with him and kept my opinions to myself.

I felt like an outsider in my own family. I was sure that I was not really my parents' child. There must have been a switch in the hospital where I was born. I thought I belonged to a gypsy circus family. So, one day I wrote to my grandmother to find out. She wrote back with the bad news (to me) that indeed, Stella and Jake were my real parents. In school I also felt odd because of my poor eyesight and intellectual interests.

Everything in the South was segregated then — buses, restaurants, hotels, even restrooms and water fountains. Washington, D.C., our nation's capital, was a city with a large black population. The Daughters of the American Revolution, which owned Constitution Hall barred the great black singer Marion Anderson from giving a concert there. Instead, she sang at the Lincoln Memorial on Easter Sunday before thousands. This knowledge weighed heavily on my heart when out of great financial need, I later accepted a small college scholarship from the D.A.R. I had applied for a full-tuition scholarship from another source. At the interview, when they asked me if I could attend even if I didn't get the scholarship, I made the mistake of telling them that I was determined to go to college, one way or another. A wiser student who really didn't need the money cried poor and got the scholarship that I really needed.

Mahatma Ghandi was assassinated in 1948. Did I even hear about it? Did I know who he was? Growing up in a newly constructed white suburban town in a non-political family that was just trying to survive the Depression, I knew nothing of the outside world. The only world I knew was my family, school and Sunday school. Daddy read the newspapers and listened to the news on the radio. My sister and I helped Mother with the dishes and read the funnies — Popeye, Li'l Abner, Orphan Annie, Dagwood. Books were my way of learning what was outside of our apartment.

Bat Girl

Because of my progressive myopia, I thought that someday I would be completely blind. I practiced walking around our apartment with my eyes closed in the daytime or at night in darkness, so that I would be able to navigate without sight. I couldn't tell one person from another past three feet so I was always getting into trouble for ignoring my friends or waving to strangers across the street. At Washington-Lee High School in Arlington, Virginia, I was the last girl to be chosen for any team activity because I couldn't catch a baseball or land a basketball in the hoop. Track was enjoyable because I was good at running and jumping.

The only things that saved me socially were my good legs and dancing. When dancing, the mouse I was grew wings. I dated Mormon boys because they were good dancers and the Mormon Church had a lot of dances. The only problem was that they wanted me to join the Church. My closest girlfriends turned against me when I didn't fulfill their missionary goals. I was much more interested in Buddhism and Yoga at that time even though I continued to sing in the Episcopal Church choir until I was eighteen and began studying with an opera teacher.

One day in 1943 my friends and I went to the local Air Force Base to learn how to spot airplanes as part of the civilian war effort. I could barely tell one silhouette of an airplane from another on the wall chart, much less in the air. This was another thing I couldn't do. My poor vision was making life difficult.

The first day of Algebra class was also very frustrating. I couldn't tell x from y on the blackboard while sitting in the center of the front row. I went to my parents in tears telling them that I must have glasses. After leaving the optometrist's office with glasses that were as thick as a Coca Cola bottle, I saw things I had never seen before – the texture of the bark on the trees and individual blades of grass. The world was more fascinating and beautiful than I had ever known — how much I had been missing. But when I looked into a mirror I saw my ugly acne-pitted face covered by thick glasses and my teeth covered with braces that were to stay on until my college years. (All the dentists had been drafted so there were no dentists available for civilians.) I had grown round shouldered from years of bending over to read or draw. You'd think my parents would have noticed that I couldn't see but mother couldn't see past her nose either and Daddy was gone much of the time. I thought that I was the ugliest person in the entire school.

    High school English was fun and funny with Miss Aldrich, her short, generous body stuffed into her clothes. She was always adjusting her bra and girdle when she lectured on Shakespeare. I liked Latin and spent many hours at home painting an illuminated oversized page of the Lord's Prayer in Latin. It was framed and hung in the classroom. Botany was the most interesting subject to me. The teacher, Lena Artz, was tall and thin with short grey hair. She invited me and my friends to spend a weekend at her cabin at a lake in the mountains where we enjoyed canoeing. She also enlisted me in the Smithsonian's project on collecting and classifying all the plants of the Washington, D.C. area. I worked on goldenrods. My mother was very tolerant of the stacks of plants pressed between layers of newspaper in my room, especially since she suffered greatly from hay fever.

    The Smithsonian's specialist in grasses, a short, slight woman with a head of pale hair that looked like dried grass, examined my work. After her approval I presented my paper at a meeting of the Cosmos Club in Washington, D.C. That was my first presentation of an academic paper before a scholarly group. Though I did not pursue a career in botany my interest was reflected in my art and the many drawings of flowers that I made since childhood. In the 1960s I made a series of drawings of ovaries of flowers that reminded me of the drawings of Matisse. In the 1970s I made fetish-like fiber sculptures by wrapping yarn around dried Century Plant flowers. I gave these "Love Branches" to friends and developed several series of wrapped fetish-like forms. A later series of paintings, *The Secret Language of Plants,* returned to a botanical theme.

Miss Elsea, a short stocky woman with short straight hair, taught physics. She was enthusiastic about machines and taught the mechanics of automobiles and steam engines. I wasn't interested and received my only B in high school. Now I find physics one of the most interesting fields of study. At graduation, I was the salutatorian and my friend Claudia Richmond was the valedictorian. She was one of the few other Claudia's I have met.

After school activities were much more interesting than the classes. The music program, directed by Florence Booker, was outstanding. I sang in the girl's chorus, floating in a sea of harmony. High points were singing in the beautiful Pan-American Building in D.C. and trips for performing in Williamsburg and Norfolk, Virginia.

And of course there were parties and dances. One Friday night after a party my friends dropped me off across the street from the apartment where I lived. I stepped out of their car and they drove on. As I crossed the street, I saw the blur of a car's lights coming toward me. I knew that it would hit me. It knocked me down. I got up and the driver got out of his car. Are you all right he asked? I brushed myself off and said I was ok, I just live right here. He drove on and I went upstairs. My mother was shocked when she saw my skinned knees and arms. She helped me clean up and I went to bed.

The next day my friend and I went on a bicycle ride of twenty miles to Tyson's Corners, then a country crossroads, now one of the busiest intersections in the United States. We bought soda pop and candy bars and then rode home on roads bordered with forsythias, past meadows of blooming coreopsis, a sunlit path of green and yellow.

I was grateful that the car had not killed me. A scar on my right hand is a reminder that any day could be my last day. I have never forgotten that moment of the blurred headlights coming at me with inevitability. Even though I always made plans for my future, I have tried to live each day as if it might be my last. Decades later that moment was reenacted with a more positive outcome when I performed with a slow moving car in the La Mamelle Gallery in San Francisco on September 11, 1977. In that performance I moved over and around the car with photographic projections and live and recorded music composed by Leonard Ellis.

When I was in high school, my first job was teaching dance in an after school program sponsored by the Hedi Pope School of Dance in Alexandria, Virginia. Miss Pope hoped that her program could be integrated into the school's curriculum along with other arts. In 1948, to celebrate my graduation from high school, my parents gave me a matched set of monogrammed leather suitcases. Was that a hint to leave home, I thought. I certainly wanted to. The suitcases were beautiful and lasted through many travels. At first my trips were just to New York City on holidays to visit the Museum of Modern Art, the Metropolitan Museum and to take modern dance classes at the Jose Limon, Charles Weidman and Martha Graham studios.

During my undergraduate years in college, I lived at home in Arlington and worked to support myself while attending the George Washington University and Corcoran School of Art in Washington, D.C. Part-time jobs were teaching dance after school during the week and teaching children's painting classes at the Corcoran School of Art on Saturdays; office jobs at the university admissions office; and summers as a camp counselor or research assistant at the Pentagon. Working and going to school didn't leave much time for social activities. I didn't have time to make connections with my peers and my parents knew nothing about the arts. Because I had no mentors, I had to learn by my mistakes as I went along in the arts because I had no mentors.

Camp Romaca for Girls was a tent camp in Maryland on the Chesapeake Bay where I taught dance and drama one summer. Perhaps the girls had fun but I was miserable. It was so hot that I swam every day and suffered from a sinus infection the whole summer. There were so many mosquitoes that there was no rest. One night not one of the girls in my tent could sleep. So we all had a great time that night skinny-dipping in the Bay. The cooling water washing over our hot skins under the stars was exhilarating. Of course someone snitched and the camp director chewed me out the next day. It didn't matter because the experience was so beautiful.

In the fall I was back to GWU where my classes in "Foggy Bottom" ended a few minutes before my painting classes started at the Corcoran School of Art. Roller skates were faster than running or taking the bus. Arriving at the Corcoran, I punched my time card; this was how the student's hours in the studio were tracked. The instructors demonstrated and made assignments on Monday. We students were on our own in the studios until Thursday when the teachers came back to critique our work.

At the University, I acted in the Theatre Department's productions directed by William Vorenberg. I was always so sensitive and easily angered or saddened. When I studied acting I learned to step outside myself in the midst of extreme emotion, to prolong the feelings in order to understand and remember them so that I could recall the emotions later on for artistic purposes. When I was crying about something at home, I would try to really go into the feelings. At the same time, part of me was observing the triggers, the emotions and the bodily sensations that were happening. When acting, I could recall experiences that helped me get into the character I was playing. With all this preparation it is ironic that the only part I remember playing in college was dancing down the aisle in a very hot gorilla suit.

Ushering in the local theatres was a job that furthered my education. It was an opportunity to see many foreign movies and plays. French movies helped me learn French. I also ushered at the new Arena Stage Theatre where I saw repeated performances of Menotti's operas. Many years later when I was the choreographer for UCLA's Opera Workshop I worked on Menotti's *Amahl and the Night Visitors.*

At the University I danced in the Dance Production Group directed by Elizabeth Burtner. I suffered greatly from stage fright, and during performances, from fear of falling or running into other dancers. Contact lenses were becoming available but at great expense and discomfort. They were quite large and out of the price range for a student. I heard about Alan Bates *Sight Without Glasses*. I bought the book and diligently practiced the exercises without any improvement in my vision.

The dance studio was in Building J. I thought the dull green paint on the studio door needed painting in a brighter color. So, one weekend I painted the door a bright orange. I thought it was much improved but most people were very shocked and the door was repainted shortly after in the dark green that matched all the other doors on campus.

Can you Draw me?

My sister Shirley answered the *Can You Draw Me* ad in the newspaper and won a scholarship to Abbott Art School in Washington, D.C. As soon as she graduated, she married her art teacher and they had a daughter. Her husband didn't want any responsibility. He hid bills under the couch and threw the baby across the room. Fortunately the baby landed on the couch.

Shirley's husband was a World War II veteran who kept a loaded German Luger in the house. One evening, when Shirley was preparing dinner, she felt like stabbing him with the butcher knife. Afraid of her potential violence added to his, she took the baby and left him. She quit art school and became a successful commercial artist.

I didn't answer that ad. At the Corcoran School of Art I took one course in commercial art and hated it. Drawing grocery, furniture and appliance ads was of no interest to me. The only assignments to my liking were textile and clothing designs where I could be creative by using my painting skills on designs related to my interest in fabrics.

Many years later, when I lived in Stinson Beach, Elizabeth Penniman, a curator, asked me to be in a self-portrait exhibition sponsored by the Bolinas Museum. The idea of looking at my face in the mirror every day for an extended period of time wasn't appealing. I preferred younger models. My first thought was to show the pastel portrait I did on my fiftieth birthday. But that was too depressing. I thought about doing an assemblage of personal objects. That would be more symbolic, more abstract and therefore more interesting. Then I remembered that I had a new blank book.

For the next two months I recorded my thoughts and sketches for a self-portrait in that square blue book. It became a daily journal. On April 23, 1993, I wrote, "Cesar Chavez died today. The sky cried. They had a mass and sang songs for him." I wondered, when I am gone, will anyone sing songs for me? My husband, Harold commented on one of the sketches, "You look like some artist ready to take a flying leap into the rolling donut hole – or something."

I sketched my face in sorrow and stillness, as my mother, as my grandmother. I covered my face with grease paint and made ten face prints. They attracted gnats, ants and self-descriptive words: left-handed, blind visionary, old child, wounded healer, dream dancer.

I love motion and resist fixing moments in time. I don't like to have my photograph taken or my voice recorded. In my drawings, an open network of lines records a series of moments by layering paths of motion. Much of my art has to do with motion. People say an artist's work is self-reflective. If we are each the model, why even hire another person to pose? Is it to avoid looking in the mirror? Can I draw me?

Shirley & Claudia Chapline
1939

Shirley Josephine Chapline, 1948
(Sister)

George Flemming Chapline II
(Half Brother)

Neal "Petey" Chapline Swalm, 1979
(Half Sister)

Claudia Chapline, *Family*, acrylic on linen, 4 feet by 8 feet.

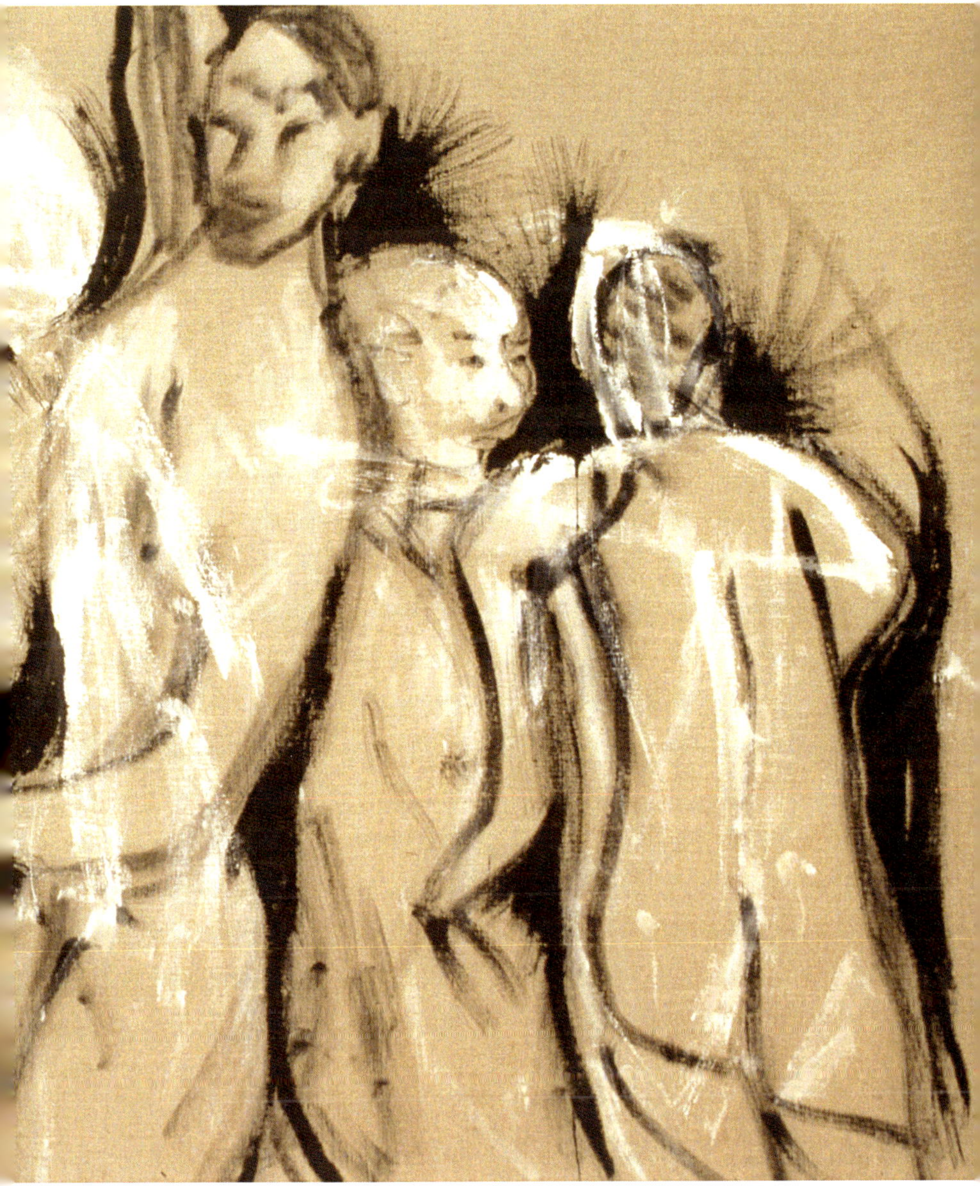

Jacob's Ladder

"Travel light," he said. Yes, Jake had choices. He was a dignified Southern Colonel type, a civil engineer, inventor, and real estate investor. He always said "Never ask anyone to do anything for you that you can do for yourself." He made himself up every morning like a bed with hospital corners, always clean, ironed and mended. In his youth he had played the banjo in a circus band at Ringling Brothers in Sarasota, Florida, where he designed the lighting system. He had managed a coal mine in Texas and built bridges and dams. Before the crash of 1929 he wore silk shirts with diamond cufflinks. After he lost his construction business, he wore cotton shirts with gold cufflinks. Then he found government jobs with the FHA and moved from place to place with the satisfaction of supporting his family during difficult times. Nothing confined him, not wealth, not poverty, nor his two wives and six children.

Now it was 1949 and I was eighteen. Jake lay in an oxygen tent thinking about his past. The country had changed a lot in his lifetime and he'd done his share to make things happen. His new invention for laying hot asphalt cold was really ticking. A couple of weeks more work and the production model would be perfected. "What the hell am I doing in this bed?" he shouted. A nurse walked in. "There's nothing wrong with my heart. I just had acute indigestion. All I need is a good crap! NO, I don't want your Goddamn bedpan! Where's the toilet? If you don't tell me I am going home this minute." So Jake, ignoring his chest pain, climbed out of the cloudy oxygen tent. He walked down the hallway with clenched teeth, entered the lavatory and closed the door.

Privacy's important to a man's dignity, he thought. The killing pains were in his arms now. He sat down on the toilet. Gasping for breath, he fell against the lever, flushing the toilet and leaving his body. Was it strength and independence or just plain stubbornness that took him away from us?

    At Daddy's funeral I met for the first time my half-sisters from Daddy's first marriage: Peggy Chapline McDonnell (Baby) and Neal Chapline Swalm (Petey), and learned about my deceased oldest half-sister, Alice Chapline Hodge (Big). My half-brother George Fleming Chapline (Chap) was also there. During childhood we had often seen our "Uncle George," since he managed a music store in Washington, D.C. George had wanted to be an opera singer, but he was encouraged to follow the family tradition and go to West Point. I remember a picture of him looking very handsome in his uniform. After graduating he managed a music store, sang solos in churches on Sundays and became an alcoholic, like our father. George had a daughter, Arden Lee by his first marriage and a son, David, by his second wife, who he married twice. At the gathering in our apartment after Daddy's funeral, George sang old songs and Petey played the piano. The gathering was sad and festive at the same time.

Petey

    I liked Petey immediately. She was a writer of stories and family history, a former journalist who created adventures that she wrote about for *Life Magazine* with her husband, Todd Swalm, a photographer. Petey was the first woman to canoe across the Okefenokee Swamp in Florida. She wrote about it and Todd photographed it. She was also an honorary Marine in World War II for *Molly's Boots*, her radio program that broadcast letters to and from Marines in boot camp. She published *Molly's Boots,* and *Once Upon a Morning* about her early days in Sarasota Florida. She wrote about Jake teaching her to shoot a squirrel between the eyes when she was five. My grandfather, a circuit court judge and his wife and my father were early settlers of Sarasota, Florida. My half-brother, "Chap," was named after my father's brother, George Fleming Chapline, a lawyer and ama-teur writer, who published *Sarasota, the Beautiful: the Legend of Sara DeSoto, the Lovely Daughter of Hernando.* This story became the basis for an annual pageant in Sarasota. The Chapline family's original home, Linger Longer, is no longer.

    Petey and I began a correspondence that lasted until she died. Once, after I'd married, I visited her in Sarasota with my children. Going into the guest room, I was shocked to see a gun on the bedside table. It was loaded. Fortunately I found it before my children did. Back home, I was a "No War Toys" mom and did not allow any kind of guns. On the floor of Petey's closet there was a faded Seminole skirt with intricate patchwork. I admired it and she gave it to me. Later, in 1972, the skirt took on new life as the costume for my dance, *Prayer for Black Mesa.*

Several years after the Florida visit, I visited Petey in the mountains of Cullowee, North Carolina where she lived alone when she was in her eighties, growing her own vegetables and fruit in the spring, canning in the summer and writing in the winter. I asked her if she was ever afraid, living out in the country alone. She replied "No. Every so often I go out and practice target shooting. No one ever bothers me." She was working on a Chapline family history, *Chaplyn's Choice* (Col. Chapline's name for his Maryland property on the King James River, where he landed in 1610.) Petey was also trying to market a book of her short stories, *Tales of a Florida Cracker.*

Petey played pianos everywhere she went. When I took Petey out to lunch on that visit, she sat down at the restaurant's piano and played some old jazz tunes that made everyone in the restaurant smile. At the end of my visit, Petey gave me a copy of *Chaplyn's Choice.* I thought it would make a good television story of a white family's roots and I lent the copy to the wife of the Hollywood producer David Weinstein. Unfortunately I never got it back. Petey died a few years later and her adopted daughter Jackie Winn died before I could get another copy. Who knows when or where Petey's story of *Chaplyn's Choice* will surface?

Claudia Chapline and James Hood
December 22, 1955

James Nicol Hood
(First Husband) 1956

Claudia Chapline and Harold Schwarm
1984

Harold Schwarm
(Second Husband) 1990

A Myopic Marriage

Because she had made two dates for the same night, my roommate at Washington University in St. Louis, Shirley Morris, asked me to take her place at a psychology lecture. My first and only blind date was Jim Hood – tall, dark and handsome with large brown eyes and a quiet demeanor. That night in 1955 was the beginning of a six-months' courtship frequently interrupted by rat feeding. Jim was working on a doctorate in psychology and his dissertation chronicled his experiments on rodent learning. I was working on my master's thesis in Dance Therapy, a means of healing through movement, while also teaching dance in the Women's Physical Education Department. In December of 1955, instead of going to Europe as I had planned, I married James Nicol Hood in the University Chapel, attended by Jim's parents, my mother, my students and faculty and friends. Huston Smith, the religious scholar and writer, was teaching at Washington University then. He married us with a custom nondenominational ceremony. Howard Kelsey wrote the music and my students performed a dance I'd choreographed titled *Rose Window*. It was a beautiful beginning for what turned out to be seventeen years of unhappily married life for me. Instead of a honeymoon, we spent one night in a modest hotel. As a sign of things to come, we ate cold spaghetti the next morning.
  After he received his Ph.D., Jim accepted a fellowship for pre-medical studies at the University of Missouri in Columbia. I continued to teach at Washington University for one more year while I drove to Columbia on weekends. Our secondhand Studebaker had a cloth

roof. One hot day in July when I had all the windows open, the cloth ripped and shredded in the wind, and fragments of cotton padding and cloth fell down like a snowstorm.

That mishap was topped by a blizzard the next winter. Suddenly a car was spinning in a circle in front of me. To avoid a collision, I swerved, too quickly and spun around and landed upside down in the ditch alongside the road. As I got out of the car I saw cars in the ditches far ahead on both sides of the icy road. A man standing by the car in front of me told me to "Be patient, they are pulling out the cars in front of us."

That was enough commuting for me. At the end of the academic year I accepted a position as Instructor of Dance at the University of Missouri in Columbia, to start in the fall of 1956. Housing in Columbia was extremely limited. The only apartment we could find was a motel room with no heat. We must have spent too much time in bed to keep warm because I got pregnant, despite using birth control. At that time the diaphragm was the only conception prevention available.

Nine months quickly passed while I was teaching modern dance technique and, in my spare time, working on my paintings. On the first day of exam week at the end of the spring semester, I felt the first contractions. I knew the baby would come quickly, but Jim, the medical student who thought we had plenty of time, was slowly waking up, showering and dressing while I kept telling him to hurry. We finally got to the hospital just in time for the nurses to prepare me and rush me to the delivery room. My son Craig came into the world, ready to begin his dance on April 30, 1957. When they placed him on my belly, I said, "He is so beautiful." The doctor said, "They are all interesting." At that moment I knew the meaning of unconditional love. When I returned to my class for the final exams a few days later, my students gave me a welcome back party. Of course, they all passed with dancing colors.

    Jim had always wanted to live in California, and the following year, he was accepted at the University of Southern California Medical School. So we drove to California with Craig, then five months old. The car broke down in Riverside. I called a friend who drove Craig and me to Los Angeles to meet Jim, who had somehow coasted the rest of the way in our broken car. We spent our first year in a rented apartment with pastel-colored walls in East Los Angeles, where Jim was an intern at the Los Angeles County Hospital. His job entailed a lot of sewing up gunshot wounds on many patients who said, "My friend did it."

    Not having a California teaching credential I supported the family with whatever job I could get. As director of the Lincoln Heights Recreation Center, I checked the sandbox each morning for weapons stored for nighttime gang fights before watching the little children play. Once, the girls after-school group wanted to cook, so we made cookies. The supervisor, Lola Sadlo, criticized me because cooking was not considered a recreational activity since these girls cook at home. I remember that day because when I got home, I discovered that someone had stolen my underwear off the clothesline.

    The following year I became the director of the Shatto Drama Center where I directed children in plays – *Everyman, Madeleine, Annie Get Your Gun* – that I adapted from familiar stories. Then, at Alhambra High School I tried to teach modern dance to 60 young women with the mentally challenged and disruptive students in the rear of the gymnasium. Instruction came after roll call, and signing innumerable excuses. I felt like I spent the year making marks in little squares. My artistic life that had begun with drawing, painting, poetry and dance in childhood never diminished. I continued to study and create to maintain my skills. During these child-rearing years I was a Super Mom, taking care of the house and garden and supporting the family during my husband's ten years of higher education by teaching in colleges and universities. When the baby went to sleep I went to work on my visual art, poetry or choreography, whatever was most pressing to be realized. No wonder I was always so tired. Many women artists give up during the child-rearing years. But I could never give up making art, no matter what happened. I wanted life and art. It was eight years between my first solo exhibition in St. Louis the year I was married and my second solo exhibition in Los Angeles. I had kept working all that time, but until then, I didn't have a cohesive body of work that I felt worth showing. I painted on the same canvases for many years and wrote poetry at night.

Craig Hood with Robin the Monkey
(Eldest Son) 1969

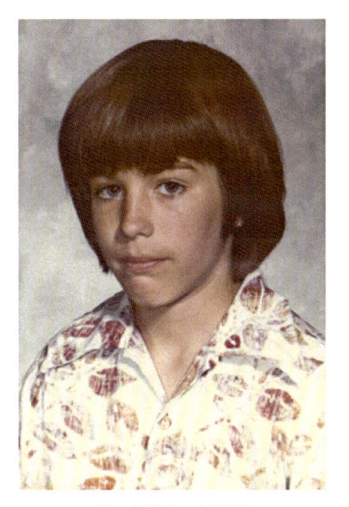

Randall Hood 1975
(Youngest Son)

Claudia Chapline with Husband and Sons, James, Randall and Craig Hood 1967
At home in Los Angeles

61

Monkey Child

My first son, Craig, was prenatally addicted to motion. Born to a dancing mother, he was athletically gifted. Nothing could confine him. When he was still in diapers, he would push chairs to the kitchen counter, climb up, eat cereal and be off over the fence and around the block before I even woke up in the morning. When he was a small boy, Craig quietly played with his toy car in a corner of Gloria Newman's Los Angeles and Anaheim studios where I studied and rehearsed Gloria's choreography for performances. When we came home, he showed me that he could do turns and jumps that he had seen in the class. He was a natural dancer, but I didn't encourage him in dance. When he got older he practiced jumping off the garage roof. Other mothers didn't want their children playing with Craig for fear they might be injured.

Craig loved animals. He was always bringing home some wild creature. He kept them for a time, and when they looked unhappy he let them go back to the woods. We had turtles, toads and snakes, also hamsters and dogs. With his spider monkey on his shoulder, Craig would pedal his bicycle off to the woods. At twelve, he practiced the flute for many hours every day and played for frogs and lizards and the monkey, named Robin Hood. Craig's breath joined the wind and flew with the birds, his sweet songs running with the waters of the creeks. Day and night his silver flute connected him to the natural world.

Robin Hood lived in a cage outside the kitchen window that was over the sink. Robin liked a lot of attention, so I talked to him while I washed the dishes. On cage-cleaning day Robin would walk around the edge of the roof eating red hibiscus flowers. It was a charming scene, until he decided to scamper up to the highest branch of a thin tree. All the neighbors' children would come around because of the noise. The tree would not support climbing so we had to trick Robin into coming down. Randy, Craig's little brother would come out with a graham cracker. Robin would swoop down to get the cracker and Craig would grab Robin, give him the treat, and put him back in his cage.

One cage-cleaning day, a neighbor's dog came up the driveway and caught Robin in his jaws, fatally injuring him. After Robin died, Craig took up surfing and became a vegetarian. Surfing gave him good lungs and a healthy appetite. When the teenage urge for independence came, he moved into the garage. He covered the walls with surfing posters and slept on a waterbed. He and his friends would project slides of waves on the white wall I had previously used for my studio paintings. Craig grew into a strong, healthy man. The sea became very important in his life. In high school he built an eighteen-foot wooden sailboat in the garage, and went on to sail it for many years. He even considered yacht design as a career, managed a yacht company and lived on his boat before changing his goal to electrical engineering. He'd found that being a yacht designer was something like being an artist: very few are able to earn a good living.

Craig met Maggie Wagoner on a sailing race from Ventura to Baja. They were married on the beach in Hawaii and had two children, Marissa and Alex. Now owner of his own electrical design company in Ventura, Craig can watch the waves from his office to know when the surfing is good. He taught Marissa to surf. She is an A student and is on the women's surf team at the University of California, San Diego. Craig and Maggie divorced and now Craig's family is his son Alex, who has a passion for golfing, and a turtle, two parakeets and Sparky, a Jack Russell Terrier.

Infant Surfer

My second son, Randall Jameson Hood came into the world on November 27, 1964, seven years after Craig was born. When Randy was only eighteen months old we went camping near the Kings River. I never liked camping out. I thought sleeping on the ground and cooking on a campfire made my life as a mother of young children even more difficult. My husband, Jim, enjoyed a relaxing time of doing nothing while I had to feed the boys without a kitchen and Craig enjoyed a chance to explore nature.

Early one morning I took Randy down by the river to wash him. He didn't want a bath. He just wanted to play in the water. What a struggle! After I soaped him up, he slipped out of my hands and into the river. I quickly grabbed onto his leg, but it was slippery and he slid out of my hand. I jumped into the river calling, "Help! Help!" The baby was floating on his back and going headfirst downstream. I caught him in a stronger hold and tried to swim to the bank. But the current was very strong and carried us downstream in a cold rush parallel to the bank. Craig came running. I shouted, "Don't get in the water." He picked up a long branch and held on tight while I struggled to reach the other end of it. I held little Randy close to my chest with my right arm and paddled with my left arm, finally catching the branch in my left hand. Then Craig pulled us up onto the riverbank.

Safe on shore and shivering, I hugged my sons in thanks. Back at the campsite, I dressed Randy and changed into dry clothes. Randy was not in the least bit upset: he had experienced an exciting river ride, and Craig was now a hero who had a wonderful story to tell his Dad when he woke up that morning. But I cried for two days. Even today I cry when I think about that day I almost lost Randy in the river. Decades after, I still have dreams about losing my baby.

Like Craig, Randy began surfing in junior high school. He and his friends cut classes when there was a swell in Malibu. After graduating from California Polytechnic University in Civil Engineering, Randall, as he now calls himself, spent a year and a half traveling around the world and surfing in Australia and Indonesia, and fulfilling his dream of surfing the Great Barrier Reef. When he came home, he showed me photographs of himself surfing waves higher than our house. "Weren't you afraid?" I asked. "Yes," he slowly said, "when you wipe out, you wipe out on coral."

Next for Randall was two years with the Peace Corps in Ecuador. Fluent in Spanish and experienced in building, he then worked for a construction company during the day and taught math and physics in the evening at the university in Guayaquil. He also acted in occasional TV spots. With his saved money, he purchased beach property in Montanita, a popular Ecuadorian surfing resort. He designed and built a surfer's hostel with fourteen rooms, a restaurant and a bar that he managed for ten years. In between solar engineering projects, he rode the waves of the Galapagos Islands. Now a father of three children, he is coming back to California with Amada, his second wife and their children, Ciara and Christopher.

Dog Stories

When I was a little girl my father used to tell stories about his hunting dog riding on the running board of his Ford, the first motorcar in Arkansas. He used to say, "The only things worth painting are beautiful women or dogs." There were pictures of pointers and setters on our dining room walls.

After my first year in art school I proudly showed Daddy the results of my life-drawing exercises. He said, "Claudia you sure got a lot of art." Well, I did, and it was all under the bed. Dogs come with children and Craig's little dog Oats chewed the corners off one hundred and fifty drawings, the blankets and the mattress. Motley was a little bit of pepper who used to chase every bitch in town, cars too. He could leap over ten-foot-high walls. That was pretty good, considering that his legs were only six inches long. The day he was run over, Craig wouldn't come down from his tree house at the top of the redwood tree in Eureka.

Now let me tell you about my dog King. King was a border collie who liked graham crackers. King got so blind and addled that he walked into a car and broke his hip. I cried for a week and became a vegetarian until I became anemic twenty-five years later.

Let me tell you about my dog Oats. Oats ran down the hill every morning to fetch the newspaper. Sometimes she brought the neighbor's paper too. She was a bit overweight but the more we tried to curtail her diet the more she charmed the neighbors out of their leftovers. And if they didn't come through, she knocked over their trashcans to get the goodies inside – old sardine cans, dog food wrappers, or popsicle sticks. But she had a most beautiful voice. She sang with the coyote chorus at night and walked with me in my dreams to the top of the mountain where she stamped her black footprints on my snow paintings.

Let me tell you about my dog.

Note: My life is reflected in my work. This story was part of the dialogue for a solo performance with dance that I performed at the Institute for Dance and Experimental Art in Santa Monica and at the Oberlin Dance Collective in San Francisco in 1976.

Claudia Chapline, *Coyote Dance from Dog Stories*
Photograph by Miklós Gyulai

Fire in Sullivan Canyon

After I separated from Jim I continued to live in the Sullivan Canyon house in the Brentwood area of Los Angeles with Randy, my youngest son. Craig had graduated from high school and gone off to Central America and I was teaching modern dance classes in my Santa Monica studio, the Institute for Dance and Experimental Art (I.D.E.A.)

On a warm September day in 1976, during the September fire season in Los Angeles County when the Santa Ana winds cause wildfires in the forests, a woman from the school called me to pick up my son. "Mandeville Canyon is on fire," she said.

Immediately I cancelled the day's classes and rehearsals and closed the studio. By the time I arrived at the Paul Revere Junior High School, horses were being evacuated from the Canyon where we lived on a little sandstone mesa. Sullivan Canyon is a small enclave of houses and riding corrals north of Sunset Boulevard on the west side of Mandeville Canyon. The road dead-ends at a bridal trail into the Santa Monica Mountains. It was an ideal place to raise boys, as long as they wore high-topped hiking boots as protection against rattlesnake bites.

When we got home that day, Randy's little black dog, Motley, was whining. He wanted to leave. Some families had already left. Those remaining were hosing their roofs. This was a moment of decision. I looked at my small Honda Civic to think what we should pack. Randy and I took turns hosing the wood shingle roof. In between turns we packed food, water, blankets, changes of clothing and two personal possessions each. Randy loaded his guitar and ski boots into the Honda. Taking my art was out of the question. I packed a briefcase with family pictures and a small suitcase with costumes, props, and audiotapes of music that had been composed for my performances. I thought that if the house burned down I could do a benefit performance to raise money for housing.

Sullivan Canyon had always seemed so safe. It had not burned in over a hundred years. Now that we were packed and ready, we decided to stay until it was absolutely necessary to leave. The fire in the adjacent Mandeville Canyon had moved north into the Santa Monica Mountains. It was very smoky but unlikely that the fire would move down into Sullivan Canyon. It was just after 5 P.M. when we took a walk to the end of the road and up the bridal trail. Several of our neighbors were already there with cocktail glasses in hand, watching the fire that was all along the ridge across the valley. It was an awesome, beautiful and frightening sight. We all hoped that the fire would be contained before reaching our canyon.

We went back to the house and hosed the roof again before dinner and uneasy sleep. We woke the next morning to the first of four days of fire fighting in the canyon, helicopter drops, smoke, heat and brave firemen who worked to extinguish the fire. An unforgettable sight was the pack of tree rats leaping from trees and across roofs as they fled the fire. We brought food and drinks to the firemen; their calm competence as they worked was reassuring. They finally succeeded in putting out the fire just four houses from mine. No one was hurt and no houses were destroyed in our small canyon. For quite some time I kept the evacuation supplies in the little Honda. And it was many years before I stopped being nervous when the hot winds of September rustled the leaves of the Sycamore trees and rattled my brain.

Claudia Chapline, *River of Fire*, acrylic on canvas, 4.5 x 18 feet

Husbands

My sister Shirley had no better luck in her two marriages than I did in my first one. Once we grew up, Shirley's life seemed to go from crisis to crisis. It was stressful to talk on the phone with her in the evenings because her bad news always disturbed my sleep. She had two unsuccessful marriages and ongoing financial troubles. Although she was a very talented commercial artist, she was not strong enough to do sustained work after being rear-ended by a City Water and Power truck in Los Angeles. She always loved babies and animals and had four children by two husbands who did not want to be fathers. Her house was filled with birds, cats, dogs, fish and love for all of them. She tried several home-based businesses for economic survival – taming jungle birds, breeding dogs, refinishing old furniture and custom painting cars. Her house, cluttered with antiques and birdcages, sounded like an aviary.

Mother, my husband and I, even my husband's parents, all tried to help her. But her troubles worsened. She became obese and suffered from osteoporosis and asthma. In her sixties she had several strokes and died at the age of sixty-five on October 10, 1996, the same day that my mother was cremated and my third grandchild, Mikaela Hood, was born.

Grandmother Hartman's husband, my grandfather, Daniel Schell, died when my mother Stella was five and her little brother, Lyle, was only three. Mother was always reticent about anything personal, so we were just told that he died, not how or when or where. In the last years of her life, I persisted in asking and finally Mother told me what had happened. She said that it was very cold, and that Daniel had gone out to the garage to warm up the car. A strong wind came up, closing the garage door; and Daniel died from carbon monoxide poisoning. After Daniel's death, Grandmother sold the farm in Michigan and moved to Oak Park, Illinois where she supported her children by running a beauty school attached to her large house.

When her children were grown, Grandmother married William Hartman. They had spent weekends together for twenty years. "Daddy Will" was always running off with other women. Then he would get sick and come back for Grandmother, who Shirley and I called Mama Lou, to take care of him. This happened too many times so Grandmother said, "If you leave me again, you are not coming back." Well, he left again and when he tried to return to Grandmother, she said "NO."

When Grandmother was in her eighties she had a lover who was ninety years old. She had retired to Florida by then. John visited her in the winter and went back to his home in Canada every summer. John's sister would come over to Grandmother's trailer and drag John home. She thought it was terrible that they were "living in sin." So John and Grandmother decided to get married. They went to their doctors for physical exams to make sure that they were both in good health. Neither of them wanted to be a burden to the other one. Then Grandmother changed her mind. She thought that if she married, she might feel obligated to go with John to Canada — and that was out of the question so she decided to keep the relationship as it was.

My own mother, Lillian Estella Scholl always married older men. I wondered if this was her way to make up for the loss of her father when she was a child. She graduated from high school at sixteen. She was five feet tall and beautiful. My father fell in love with her at first sight as she was coming home from the grocery store. He kept following her and asking her to marry him. She kept saying, "Go away, you crazy old man." He was divorced at the time and already had four grown children. Jake persisted until Stella gave in and married him when she was seventeen. He adored her and she loved him, and played her feminine role as housewife just as he played his masculine role as breadwinner and king of the house. Jake was a good provider who always had a job during the Depression. The only trouble was that every now and then he would go off on a bender for a couple of weeks, becoming very generous with friends and acquaintances and spending a lot of money on gifts. Meanwhile at home Mother was keeping the house together and stretching limited dollars to feed my sister and me. Daddy went to a dry-out clinic once that I remember, and, eventually, in his sixties, gave up drinking through Alcoholics Anonymous. My mother gave him an ultimatum saying, "I will leave you forever if you ever touch another drop of liquor." The last decade of his life was dry and peaceful. After Daddy's second and fatal heart attack when I was eighteen, Mother became a widow for the first time.

That's when Stella went to work outside the home for the first time. She was so very proud of her first job of inking maps for the national government, that she held for seven years. She was a perfectionist and very slow at a job she could handle with her near-sighted vision.

Then, while visiting Grandmother in Florida she met Frank Raines, a retired Army Colonel, who became her second husband. My mother's beauty was very attractive to men. Frank was jealous and followed her everywhere, even to the beauty parlor. She had no privacy and no time alone. He also became very mean and she began to think that she had made a mistake in marrying him. After he became sick with Parkinson's disease Stella was very responsible, caring for him at home as long as possible. When he was placed in a nursing home, she visited him every day. Meanwhile, money was running out and she didn't know what to do. One Sunday she decided to go to church and pray.

Her car and another car arrived at a parking place in front of the church at the same moment. She said, "He, being a gentleman, let me have the space. At the doorstep of the church I thanked him. This was the first time either of us had gone to that church. Afterwards he invited me out for coffee and I accepted. He was a recent widower."

He was Herman Sylvanus Boyer, and after several more church services, coffee klatches, lunches and visits with Grandmother, he asked my mother to marry him. She said that she couldn't because she was married. Herman said, "I will wait." After Frank died, Herman again asked her to marry him. Stella said, "I have to take care of my mother." Then Herman bought a house large enough for both of them and Grandmother. Several months after Mother became a widow for the second time, she and Herman were married in Orlando, Florida when I was thirty-six, and had long ago moved to California. Herman was a retired furniture dealer originally from Pennsylvania. He was an amateur geologist and designed jewelry for my mother with the stones that he collected. He also collected art and donated it to local museums. Mother and Herman had a very happy marriage. Mother told me, "He had all the good qualities of your father and none of the faults." They enjoyed twelve years of a good life together with a lot of travelling.

But everything changed in a moment when a careless neighbor accidentally struck Herman down with her car. He never recovered from that accident, which caused a blood clot on his brain. The necessary surgery left him incontinent and needing constant care for several years before my mother became a widow for the third time. After that, Stella decided not to marry again.

When Stella was eighty, she was missing male company. She liked going out to dinner and the theatre, museums and travelling. She wasn't comfortable with groups, so she signed up for a matchmaking service for senior singles. After watching a number of videotapes she interviewed three prospects. Each of them wanted a wife, someone to cook and clean house. Well, she had had enough of that. She didn't want a husband. She just wanted a playmate.

My own first husband, James Nicol Hood, was an insecure, unhappy man. He walked like a duck and had eyes like a cow. His voice was as flat as the prairie. He lived in his head and often stumbled over his untied shoelaces. Nervousness made his hands cold and sweaty and his underarms smelled of fungus. He didn't even warm up his stethoscope before putting it on a patient's chest. Needless to say, he wasn't very successful as a general practitioner, so he specialized in psychiatry. That way he didn't have to talk very much. He much preferred listening to talking. His favorite job was at a Catholic Hospital for the deaf, where he learned sign language. He was very cautious about prescribing medicine for anyone other than himself. When the nuns complained about one of his patients running down the hall and lifting the skirts of the nurses, he considered that behavior a sign of health and refused to medicate the patient.

As a doctor, he had access to all the drugs he wanted. He always had trouble sleeping, resulting in nightly masturbation when I was not available. When sex didn't work for sleeping he took Benadryl. Over the years he dulled his sensitivities so much that he couldn't walk on his own. He retired to viewing television in the daytime and smoking marijuana.

Jim and I were close in age. Both of us had fathers who'd lost their businesses in the crash of 1929. Jim's father, Louis Hood, got ulcers and gave up. His mother became a substitute teacher who entertained her students with poems by Robert Burns and stories by Mark Twain. My father worked for the government and my mother stayed at home. We both started working when we were young. I had confidence that I could always find a way to survive. Jim was also a good student, but he liked school more than I did. He wanted to be a student forever. I supported him through ten years of graduate study after his Ph.D. degree. Perhaps it was my mothering instinct that attracted me to someone so needy.

But eventually I found that his needs were unending. He drained me of all my energy, my love and my luck. Instead of my joy in life and my good luck rubbing off on him, his bad luck rubbed off on me. He was jealous of my work. He objected to my middle-of-the-night writing. He didn't understand why I couldn't write poetry in the daytime. Perhaps I slept through several years of lost poetry while trying to appease him. His constant verbal abuse was hard to take though the nearest he came to physical abuse was throwing a frying pan against the wall. I said if he ever did that again I would leave him.

I had grown up with an example of a cooperative marriage and had no brother to defend myself against as a child, so I didn't know how to fight back or stand up for myself. With Jim, I just turned the other cheek until I was psychically black and blue all over. After giving him everything possible, I learned that I could never make him happy. I had just allowed myself to become depleted by a selfish man who manipulated everyone in his family to satisfy his greed. He lied and cheated everyone, even giving the children IOUs for Christmas that were never paid.

Once we went to Jim's mentor for marital counseling. Just one session showed me that this psychiatrist's goal seemed to be helping one to adjust to a society that I was trying to change through my work with other feminist artists. My misery ended in divorce in 1974 when Jim refused to give me any money to run the house when I was disabled from a hysterectomy and unable to work. Jim thought I could teach dance when the doctor said that I should lie down to let the stitches heal. This was before laser surgery.

Though I wasted seventeen years on a mistaken marriage, my love was not wasted. I have two sons who are my pride and joy. Jim died a sad old man, with money in so many accounts that he couldn't keep track of it or enjoy it. When my children were growing up I never said anything negative about their father, although when they were older, I did caution them about the uselessness of expecting anything from him. When I married Jim, I was blind and ignorant. If we had lived together first I never would have married him. But few people did that in those days, certainly not in my traditional family. Recovering my self-esteem and financial independence took many years. It is said that what doesn't kill you makes you stronger. Fortunately I left before it killed me and eventually I became stronger. I told myself that I would never marry again unless the man came to me through my work and could cook.

Well, that's exactly what happened and so I did marry again. My second husband, Harold Chambers Schwarm, listens to my poems and sometimes contributes funny lines and illustrations for my books. An artist himself, he is the perfect art companion and a better housemate that most men. He is a low maintenance husband and the most liberated man of his generation I have ever known. He irons his own shirts and sews on buttons with needles and threads from a khaki World War II sewing kit, and best of all, he likes to cook. I only wish he liked to travel as much as I do. In fact, he hates to travel and is a terrible travelling companion. Solo travelling is preferable to listening to his complaints.

Nose in a Book
And Reflections on Writing

When I married Jim Hood we had no furniture, but we both had books. The book stacks became stools and support for a table. The books kept growing and moved from place to place. Finally, when we lived in Sacramento, I had a wall of shelves built for my books. Everything was organized. But eight years later, the books were packed into boxes for the move to Stinson Beach. Nothing has been organized since. The beach house has no wall big enough for all the books. Harold and I live with stacks of books in every room. Books have been taken out of boxes as needed and stacked. After twenty years, the stacks are still growing. Several small bookcases are overflowing. Book stacks are on chairs, tables and stools – beside the bed, under the bed, under the windows and in the closets.

For years, I left my money in the car four blocks away when visiting book stores, but often had to run back to get cash for a necessary purchase. Now I try not to buy books because the Stinson Beach library is so good. But I do pick up inexpensive reference books or examples of good design that have been donated to the library. My goal is to donate two books for every one that I acquire but even with reading every day, the stacks of books are there until the next earthquake rearranges them.

I started writing as a child to express my feelings and to understand what I was thinking. One of my poems was published in the *Washington Post* when I was nine years old. After that my mother asked me to write occasional poems for Grandmother for Mother's Day. I didn't feel right about it because it seemed like a class assignment, not a real gift from the heart, but I did it anyway. When Mother asked for a poem again I told her that I didn't write any more, although in high school I worked on the school annual and *PEN,* the literary magazine, contributing drawings and poems. Being shy and not knowing any poets, I was a closet poet for half of my life.

After graduating from high school in 1948, I wanted to study creative writing but at that time there were only two universities that offered programs— Stanford and New York University. Now there are over 350 programs in creative writing in the United States. Without any means of support, I didn't see how I could leave home. But the lack of a writer's formal education could not stop a born writer from writing. I continued to write poetry throughout my life, even though I rarely showed it to anyone for many years because of my lack of confidence.

Now I write every day, starting with notes about what is happening around me. I look out of the window and read. Word bugs sting me into greater awareness. My notes become haiku and longer poems, flash fiction, and memoirs. I delight in solving the aesthetic puzzles that arise when I attempt to make artifacts from words reflecting the chaos of life. I write because I must.

It took me many years to come to this daily work. My visual difficulties and my sensitive nature made communication with others difficult. I had no mentors. In 1951, I was assisting Marion Chace in dance therapy sessions at St. Elizabeth's Hospital in Washing-ton, D.C. I knew that Ezra Pound was there, and I had read and admired his poetry, but I didn't have the courage to try to meet him.

After moving to Los Angeles in 1957, I found a poetry community at Beyond Baroque, a meeting center in Venice, where I went to readings and workshops led by Frances Healy and James Krusoe. Beyond Baroque, founded by George Drury Smith, continues to be an important poetry center and publisher.

It wasn't until the 1970s and the Women's Movement when I was living in Los Angeles that I gained confidence in my writing and finally had the courage to publish and read my poems in public. I was able to bring my work with words together with objects and movement in art performances. I coordinated the Women's Poetry Readings at Womanspace, did art performances there and elsewhere and participated in Paul Vangelisti's poetry performance series at the Pasadena Playhouse. The photographer, Lyn Smith, and I collaborated on a book of poems and photographs, *Seasons of Love*. We sent it out to a number of publishers, but at the time it would have been a very expensive book to publish. It is just as well. I have destroyed many of those early poems.

My performances attracted the attention of other writers. One time a young man came to my house to interview me for some publication. I was so tongue-tied that I couldn't answer any of his questions. The next interview was even more of a disaster. It was to be on a KPFA radio program. I was so tired and anxious that I thought I would take a short nap before driving to the station in Santa Monica. I woke up two hours later, too late to get to the station before the program was over. Even worse in front of a camera, I would hide if I could. Eventually, I got used to being interviewed. Some interviewers are in love with their own voice and want to show off their knowledge or in television, want to make fun of their guest. I learned to plan on getting one short point across while playing the clown.

Once I began writing art reviews for the *Womanspace Art Journal*, I contributed reviews of art, dance and theatre for local alternative papers such as *Woman, L.A. Free Press, Dance West, Artists' News* and the *California Dance Educators Newsletter* that I also edited. Many of my poems that were submitted to small press journals were published. I began self-publishing my chapbooks in 1996 as accompaniments to my art exhibitions because I didn't have time to submit them to publishers for consideration. The costs on all of my publications were recovered by sales, and that earned enough on each one to publish another book.

One summer day in 2002, Laurie Stoelting, a haiku poet and editor for the Haiku Poets of Northern California, visited my gallery. She liked my brush drawings with Japanese ink and asked me to do a cover drawing for a haiku by Issa for the *Two Autumns* journal she was editing. This was my introduction to the Haiku Poets of Northern California. HPNC has since published several of my poems in their journal, *Mariposa*. They are my haiku family. The Marin Poetry Center has also supported my work by publishing some of my darker or political poems and providing opportunities for public readings.

In Stinson Beach I joined Barbara Martin's monthly First Thursday Poets gatherings where local poets share and critique current work. It has been a good venue for trying out new work and editing before submitting it for publication.

As part of my art practice I make unique books from studio fragments — poems, objects, drawings, paintings, as well as altered books from library discards, trash, old appointment books, calendars and maps. When I was about ten I made my first book at a local recreation center. Later I made Xerox books in small editions. One year I painted and wrote poems in the telephone book. That work was the start of a series of assemblages and an art performance, *The Telephone Book.*

    I tried many ways of combining words and images in drawing and painting – press-on letters, stencils, scanning. Now I like using my own handwriting for incorporating words or poems into my visual artwork because it is more compatible with my drawn lines. Some of my books become sculptural objects for the wall or pedestals.

    The books are a parallel activity along with painting, sculpture and installations. I write and paint most days. The books are small and take so long to make that many pieces are sitting around in my studio waiting for that special something to add for completion, or for me to have the patience and energy to put all the little pieces together. Some tedious projects I work on a little each day, page by page, until the book is done. For example – paint each page, glue something on each page, write something on each page, and fold, sew or glue it all together. All together the books are a kind of diary of making art.

    Several years ago, I started to write an autobiography. I wrote from the beginning and tried to keep events in chronological order. But once the doors of memory were opened, years, events and people became entangled and confused, especially after the bag containing my journal was stolen in 2009. My family and my work are intermingled. Shifting into reverse, colorful shadows float. The years' events rewind. Sliding back lost objects surface, the past links to the present.

I went in one door and out another. During this moment of distraction, my bag was stolen from a dark corner in my gallery. Someone who doesn't love words and images walked away with photographs lodged in the camera, a long life in a small book of lined pages, memories of past years carefully recorded in a worn journal. I mourned lost stories, drafts of poems never to be heard or read, fragments of thoughts unrealized. Without my pictures and words who am I?

At the time, I thought my attachments were detached forever, but then I became humbled once more. To protect my words now, I carry them in my head. I am a writer when I write. The words on paper were breaths that carried moments in a changed place. With my past stolen I could be free — if I stopped looking for my bag. That thief stole my peace of mind, pieces of my heart. Suspicious of every stranger, I started hiding things and forgot where they were. I had to reorganize my life to find myself. Trying to remember a lost story, to feel the emotion that propelled it was impossible. I remembered an ending, but not how to begin the river of words that ran out to the sea. Living had changed the story. I needed to begin the book again.

For a year I was stuck. I didn't know where I was in the story of my life. Did I write this before? Am I repeating myself? Little stories kept creeping up that didn't fit into a neat sequence. They seemed more interesting than the chronological narrative. Together they formed a collage of my life and art, like turning a magnifying light on facets of a cut gemstone. Life passed by. The autobiography turned into a memoir. Just as I was getting into it again, my computer crashed in May of 2010. The internal backup also crashed and a very expensive data recovery was unsuccessful.

More life intervened. To be more specific, there was car trouble, moving my office and an IRS audit. With short-term memory going, long-term memory kicked in to jumpstart a new beginning. During the move I found hard copies of all but three poems in *Sea Glass*, the poetry manuscript that was ready to go to the printer when the computer died. Of course, in retrospect, the lost poems seemed to be the best. After reentering *Sea Glass* in the computer, I published it in September of 2010. In 2011 I worked on other poetry manuscripts and in late October was ready to start again on the memoir, working toward completion in 2012.

While writing this memoir I wandered in the field of memories like a hummingbird flitting from blossom to blossom of salvia, sucking drops of nectar. Poems were jumpstarted from an unexpected flight of small birds, or pebbles of words stumbled upon. I walked about not seeking, just awake to looking and listening. In the morning a blue heron stood on the dock, watching. A sea otter poked his head out of the water. I sipped green tea. The fog lifted its grey curtain, yellowing.

Reading and writing have always saved me from boredom, frustration, despair, incapacity and illness. I wrote when I couldn't dance or paint. I wrote in closets and bathrooms, in airports and hotels, in the middle of the night and early in the morning before first light. I wrote for pay and for play, forsaking conversation and other amusements. Now I write first and at the end of the day. Writing has helped me to look longer and to think more deeply, to listen more carefully and to connect with others. Through public readings, publications and exhibitions my writing and art are my connections to the world.

Learning to See

As time speeds up and my teeth grow long, losses pile up like fallen leaves in autumn. Invitations to memorial services and celebrations of life come as frequently as doctor's appointments. I begin reading the obituaries in the newspapers, looking for people I know. With loss of energy I travel less often and for shorter distances. I find myself asking, is this trip worth the trouble, the expense and the energy? Sleep seems less a waste of time now and more a necessary restorative, even if it comes in shorter lapses.

When my gray hairs finally outnumbered the brown, people offered to help me cross the street or carry my packages. Was it because I was slow or because my normal look of curiosity appeared to be confusion? I am always looking at everything surrounding me. This new helpfulness of strangers seemed a threat to my independence. Were they looking for someone to assist as their good deed for the day? Now, instead of feeling guilty for attracting their attention I thank them for their assistance and feel happy to have helped to make their day.

I spend more time at my gallery than ever before. I paint more with black, gray and white than with other colors. A fog inside is growing to meet the coastal fog outside my door. As people enter the gallery, I can't distinguish their features, instead, recognizing them from their voices and their movements like I did when I was a child. Finally it becomes dangerous to drive. The cataracts on my eyes are obscuring my vision. That's when I knew it was time and worth the risk of blindness to have corrective surgery.

How lucky I feel to live in this time of medical technology. At age sixty-five, I was able to do something about my vision that was getting worse every day. The outpatient laser surgery to replace my eye's lenses with plastic lenses was an experience of prismatic beauty. And after, to see the world again with full light, color and depth, was a daily miracle. My vision now is the best in my life. I am grateful to see clearly on waking up every morning.

The Cycle of Life

My eyes also opened to tragedy. Just after recovering from the cataract surgery, my niece Sharon called to tell me that my sister Shirley was in the hospital with a blockage in her leg. Shirley had previously had several small strokes so there was great concern. Then, while in the hospital, she had another stroke, which left her blind and speech impaired. I bought an air ticket to Burbank and packed my bags to leave the next day. Then my mother's caretaker called to tell me that my mother had died in her sleep.

After eighty-two years, the woman who could not stop talking was now silent. I changed my ticket to Daytona, Florida to take care of my mother's remains and affairs. She was as beautiful in death as in life, and I believe she willed herself out of her body. She was determined to remain independent, to always take care of herself. She also thought that the worst thing would be to outlive her children.

Shirley and Mother had always been very close, as connected in death as they were in life. The phone in Mother's apartment was ringing when I returned from her cremation. It was Sharon informing me that Shirley had died that afternoon. Everything changed all at once, no longer the big sister, I was now the elder of the family. The next call that came in that day was from my son Randall. Mikaela Camilla Hood, my third grandchild, was born on that same day, October 10, 1999. I left the next day for Burbank, California to attend my sister's cremation. Then I spent the next year creating a memorial exhibition for my mother, *Stella's Kitchen,* which was presented by the Bolinas Museum.

Of all the jobs I have had, motherhood was the most difficult. The joy of conception, the anticipation and growth of the fetuses that were to become my sons, and the births of my sons were just the beginning. That was the easy part. After the creative period, there came the labor of caring for them as infants, getting to know them and guiding them as children, helping them through youthful changes, letting them go as they emerged into early adulthood. At the same time, I lost myself in them. After so many years of considering them first, I eventually had to find myself again. Who was I and what did I want to do now that I was free and on my own?

The years flew by and my sons came back to me with their wives and children. Now I experience the joy of watching the grandchildren grow and challenge themselves; I enjoy the giving and receiving of love without the day-to-day responsibility for their nurturing. Parenting was good, but being a grandmother is better. I don't miss the diaper changes, the sicknesses, the accidents, the temper tantrums or dealing with their adolescent experiments and ventures into the world. I remember fondly my sons' learning to walk and to speak, their first drawings, home runs and graduations, even the tennis shoes in the middle of the floor that were once a source of irritation. I wish that I'd had more energy when my sons were small so that I could have enjoyed them as much then as I do now.

Everyone wants love, to be the recipient of love. My parents were good people and responsible but I never felt loved. Though I loved my friends I never felt that they loved me. I had respect from my students and colleagues but not love. I loved my first husband but he did not love me. I don't think I was deficient in giving but I was deficient in perception, a kind of seeing. Only in my later years do I feel a great sense of being loved – by my second husband, my sons and grandchildren and my friends. My life has been one of loving and now I feel grateful for the love that comes *to* me as well as *through* me.

Falling Up The Stairs

It has been many years since that summer of scabby knees in Lynchburg, Virginia where I learned to roller skate in the city of many hills. I get dizzy on ladders and staircases. When I look out of skyscraper windows or get near the edge of a cliff my knees get wobbly and my stomach spins. I do not ride on an escalator if I can find an elevator, but I don't like glass elevators on the outsides of buildings. To walk on a freeway overcrossing, I shut my eyes and hold tightly to the railing. I may have fallen more or less often than other people, and I have never been seriously hurt when I fell. The only broken bones I have had were not from falling, but from trying to move a heavy desk without wearing shoes – it slipped on the wood floor and crushed my right big toe. I was a dancer then and wondered how I would stand on my right foot without the use of my big toe, so I meditated on the pieces of bone growing back together, and so they did.

In school I was always tripping on something, falling up the stairs, the contents of my purse and my books scattered all over the staircase. And, on my first day of travelling anywhere, I usually trip on a curb or cobblestone while looking at the sky or an interesting building. In Berlin, my new pants were torn at the knee when I fell on the sidewalk, and I fell in San Miguel de Allende while looking for a sun-hat that wouldn't fall off my small head. I stubbed my toe in Las Vegas and people helped me get up. While I was rushing to mail a letter in Osaka, I tripped on a loose electrical cord from another artist's installation, hurting my left knee and left wrist. This made things very difficult. Imagine trying to eat noodle soup with a pair of chopsticks in your non-dominant hand.

At the College Art Association conference in New York one February, I didn't slip on the black ice, but I did fall down a long escalator. I was carrying too many books and lost my balance and fell. The corners of the steps hit my lower right leg all the way down. Trying to stand only resulted in more scratches and bruises. Someone yelled, "Sit down" and I sat down. Finally arriving at the lower level, I stepped off and picked up my books. Now that part of my leg has large varicose veins, is reddish in color and sometimes swells up.

I even fall at home. Bending over to pull up a weed I trip on a rock, and fall on my knees. And then, there are the occasional episodes of vertigo, an inner ear imbalance. I have to remind myself not to change my head position too fast, to allow my body to adjust to changes of level. Severe spells, with the walls spinning, necessitate using a cane to keep from falling.

Like one of those Japanese rocking dolls, I always come back up after a fall. I do the same with failure and rejection. Failure is a learning process, a necessary step toward the next version of a project. I used to suffer so much while trying for perfection, but finally learned when to stop. The same goes for rejection. I have learned where my work doesn't fit and continue the search for the right place for the work. In the past, I threw my best work out the window of opportunity. Sometimes, a preservationist caught it. More often it was lost in a storm or landed in a recycle bin or compost heap. Soon the window sash will break, the hinges will rust and the window will close. Falling often has taught me to walk more carefully, and to look ahead.

Home

    We create homes as a second skin to protect and insulate the body. I have had many such homes. Some were a reasonably good fit, others not so good. Home was once where Mother and Daddy were. The pristine and formal apartment in Arlington, Virginia was like a stage set for a play that never happened. As a child I preferred the cluttered house of my friend, Joan Higginson, where people were coming and going and things were happening.

    When I graduated from George Washington University, I had never lived away from home, so I accepted the job offer in St. Louis and never went back to Arlington. After growing up in the soft green light and rolling hills of Virginia, I was never happy living inland. I didn't appreciate the flatness of the land. I desired variety and felt that the sameness that comforted Midwesterners was monotonous. But the studio where I danced or painted was always home, regardless of the landscape around me.

    Los Angeles became my next home for twenty-five years. It took ten years for me to get used to the harsh light and contrasting dark shadows, the agave's knife-like leaves, the prickly pear needles and the palm trees that dusted off the chalk-gray sky as it turned rose, purple and orange at dusk. The pastel colors of the houses were amusing. We lived on a little sandstone mesa in Sullivan Canyon where my children were happy sliding down the mountain opposite on cardboard and exploring the hills of the Santa Monica Mountains State Park.

    After the divorce and the children had grown, I

lived for eight years in a Victorian country house in the center of Sacramento that I bought in a probate sale. This was a dream home in terms of space, convenience and the old furniture that came with it. This home fulfilled my desire to bring an old house back to life. However the climate did not agree with me, and the pollution from cars and rice burning that sits in that valley aggravated my asthma, and I got chronic bronchitis and pneumonia. I had to get back to the coast for my health.

When first driving on Panoramic Highway to Stinson Beach, I felt like I was a young girl again, going to summer camp in Virginia. I still feel that way after twenty-five years of driving that beautiful winding road. For a number of years before I moved to Stinson Beach, I had dreamt of a little green village where the mountains met the sea. I had painted the curve of the beach many times before I ever actually saw it.

Now I feel so fortunate to see every morning the great blue heron, snowy egrets, the night heron, and the kingfisher perched on his lookout branch. Clean air, good water and access to locally grown organic food are precious gifts these days.

My house has small rooms with high ceilings. In the past I had large studios away from home. The small home studio I now share with my husband has taught me the discipline and joy of finishing. No longer are ten works in progress lying about. Now I have to finish what I am working on to make room for the next project. Working at home has also made me more productive. There is no time wasted in commuting and I often work late into the night.

There is also the community of Coastal Marin – a gathering of artists, writers, and environmentalists, and musical, literary and painting groups. Stinson Beach, with its population of perhaps a thousand people, is the smallest town I have ever lived in, and it is the only place where I have felt connected to a community. The Coastal Health Alliance has provided me with the best medical care I have ever had. They have saved my life three times. The Stinson Beach Library also has the best service, and for a writer, library access is most important.

I love the dynamics of the coastal environment. The moving fog is so unlike the static tule fog of the Sacramento Valley. The constant sound of the surf, the egret's squawk, the rush of wings overhead, the diamond-like sparkling of the light, the many colors of the sea — even the mating sounds of the raccoons who keep trying to make their home under my house, fill me with nature's abundance and the connection to all things in time and space. None of my many homes has been as satisfying as the little house in Stinson Beach. This is the home I dreamed of all my life. Here I feel at home in my body, in my house, and in my community, knowing that it is all as transient as the fog that flows over Mount Tamalpais.

Dear Marissa,

Two days after your birth I held you in my arms and saw an old soul. You can see things and create anything. You made your own space ship. You covered the patio with chalk drawings and filled a wall with your art. You made toys for your little brother. It has been a pleasure to see you grow up into such a beautiful woman.
Love,
Nana

Dear Alex,

At my house in Stinson Beach, you took my hand and said your first sentence, "Nana, will you come down and play with me?" Later you played baseball and now golf. You see everything and say very little. Your grandfather didn't talk very much either. Often, I wonder what you are thinking. I don't say much either. It is easier for me to write than to speak, so it is hard for us to have much of a conversation. Harold says the same thing about me. There is an old saying, "Still waters run deep." Maybe we are deep in thought or just enjoying the daily spectacle of whatever is happening.
Love,
Nana

Dear Miki,

The distance between us is so great. I have missed seeing you since your visit last summer. I am hoping that you will be able to spend your high school years with your Father and his family in Southern California. You are so smart and I am very proud of your success in school.
Thinking of you every day with much love,
Nana,

Dear Miki, Ciara and Chris,

You lived so far away in Ecuador during your earliest years. Looking at your photographs every day, I wonder how you are doing. You are moving to California as I write this letter. Soon we will have the chance to see and get to know each other better. At the new year, we will all be grateful to be together again.
I love you,
Nana

Coat of Arms

Our Family Tree

CLAUDIA B. CHAPLINE — MOTHER

JAMES NICOL HOOD — FATHER

LILLIAN ESTELLA SCHELL — GRANDMOTHER

JACOB BURWELL CHAPLINE II — GRANDFATHER

FRANCES KINSMAN — GRANDMOTHER

LOUIS CHARLES HOOD — GRANDFATHER

LEUZETTA BEECHUM — GREAT-GRANDMOTHER
DANIEL SCHELL — GREAT-GRANDFATHER

Alice Hodges Chapline — GREAT-GRANDMOTHER
JACOB BURWELL CHAPLINE — GREAT-GRANDFATHER

JANE WRIGHT NICOL — GREAT-GRANDMOTHER
THOMAS HENRY KINSMAN — GREAT-GRANDFATHER

CECILIA GRINSER — GREAT-GRANDMOTHER
CHARLES LAWRENCE HOOD — GREAT-GRANDFATHER

Claudia Chapline Chronology

1930	Born May 23, Oak Park, Illinois, USA
1936-7	Moved to Washington, D.C., Newport News, St Petersburg and Lynchburg, VA
1938	Moved to Arlington, Virginia
1948	Graduated from Washington-Lee High School, Arlington, VA, Salutatorian
1949-1953	Apprentice to Marion Chace, St. Elizabeth's Hospital, Washington, D.C. B.A. Geo. Washington University, Washington D.C. Drawing & Painting, minor in Speech & Drama, Cum Laude, Special Honors in Art, PBK
1954 & 1956	Summers, Connecticut College School of Dance, New London, CT
1954 1957	Dance Instructor, Washington University, St. Louis, MO
1955	Married James Nicol Hood, First solo exhibition, Humanist Center, St. Louis, MO
1956	M.A., Health & Physical Education (Dance Therapy,) Washington University
1957	Birth of first son, Craig Chapline Hood Dance Instructor, University of Missouri, Columbia, MO. Moved to Los Angeles
1964	Birth of second son, Randall Jameson Hood
1957-1972	Taught dance and drama at various schools and colleges in the Los Angeles area Assistant Professor of Dance, California State College (CSUN,) Northridge, CA Assistant Professor of Dance, University of California, Los Angeles, CA Performed with Instant Theatre, Gloria Newman, Richard Oliver Dance Cos.
1965	Director/Choreographer, *The Mother of Us All*, UCLA Opera Workshop
1966	Camped on the Hopi Reservation
1967	Moved to Eureka, CA. showed at Hobart Gallery

1968	Moved back to Los Angeles, showed at Humboldt Galleries, San Francisco, CA
	Solo exhibition at Crocker Gallery of Art, Sacramento, CA
1973	Founded Claudia Chapline Dance Theatre Company, Santa Monica, CA
	Solo Exhibition, Jacqueline Anhalt Gallery, Los Angeles
1974-1975	Co-Founder Womanspace and Women's Building, Los Angeles, CA
1974	Divorced James Nicol Hood; Event, World Crafts Council, Toronto, Ont. Canada
1974-1982	Founder/Dir., Institute for Dance and Experimental Art, Santa Monica, CA
1976	Comprehensive Employment Training Act Performance Art Project, Introductions at Downey Museum of Art, Downey, CA
1980	California Arts Council, New Arts Series Grant for I.D.E.A.
1982-1989	Arts Administrator, California Arts Council, Gray Whale Gallery, Sacramento, CA
1987-2011	Claudia Chapline Gallery, Stinson Beach
1989	Married Harold Chambers Schwarm
1990-2011	English Language Escort, United States Department of State
1994-2010	International Exhibitions in Europe, Latin America, and Asia
1998	"Stella's Kitchen," Bolinas Museum, Bolinas, CA
1999	Artist in Residence, Recology, San Francisco, CA
2002	Curator, San Francisco/Paris Exchange, Somarts Gallery, San Francisco, CA
2003	Biennale Internazionale Dell'Arte Contemporanea, Florence, Italy
2006	Lifetime Achievement Award, Northern California Women's Caucus for Art
2009-2012	Co-Founder/Pres. Art at the Cheese Factory, Novato, CA

Acknowledgements

My thanks to all who helped me in my journey, my teachers and friends, from the Sunday painter in the park who gave me my first oil painting lesson to my husband, Harold Schwarm, who listens to my writing, critiques my art and makes the best eggs for breakfast. For their encouragement and reading of some of these stories or poems special thanks go to Lawrence DiStassi, Jim Kravets, Jacqueline Kudler, Joyce Lynn, Adam David Miller, Doreen Stock, Jyoti Wind and the First Thursday Poets of Stinson Beach — Lynda Beigel, Sandra Cross and Barbara Martin, to Katie Kukulka for preparation of the photographs, and especially to Frances Lefkowitz for her encouragement, inspiring teaching, and careful editing of this book.

Earlier versions of some of the stories were first published in the following publications:

Excerpts from "A Nuclear Family," Point Reyes Light, December 20, 2012

"When my hair turned gray," *Unraveling Mysteries,* Anthology ed. Jyoti Wind, 2011

"Can You Draw Me," (Sketches for a Self-Portrait,) *Self Portraits: True Stories,* Bolinas Museum Catalog, 1993

Excerpts from "Home" *North Coaster*, Point Reyes Light, Point Reyes Station, CA, Summer, 2012

"Reflections on Writing," *The Creative Arc*, ed. Jyoti Wind, Starshine Publications, Boulder, CO